Memoirs of a River...
...Up the Crystal©

PEOPLE & PLACES IN THE CRYSTAL RIVER VALLEY

VOLUME ONE

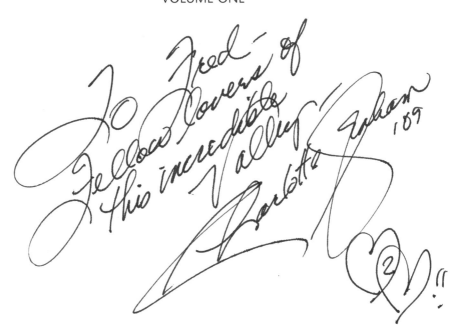

To Fred ~
Fellow lovers of
this incredible
Valley
Charlotte Graham
'09

Published by CreateSpace, dba of On-Demand Publishing, LLC
ISBN 1442170794
EAN 9781442170797
Library of Congress Control Number: 2009909891

Cover: Nelly Belle, a 1929 Model A Ford driven by owner, Gene Hill,
with author, Charlotte Graham as a passenger, heading up the Crystal River Valley,
Whitehouse Mountain in background. Photograph by Doug Whitney.

*To Doug
the breath of life,
You are to me*

TABLE OF CONTENTS

Introduction   1

Chapter 1 – The First People in the Crystal Valley   5

Chapter 2 - Redstone's General Store   11

Chapter 3 - Filoha Meadows   19

Chapter 4 - BRB Resort-Rock Creek Schoolhouse   27

Chapter 5 - Satank   33

Chapter 6 - Thompson Homestead/Sustainable Settings   37

Chapter 7 - Swiss Village Resort   43

Chapter 8 - Marble Memorial Airport   51

Chapter 9 - Marble Sheep Run   57

Chapter 10 – Marble's God-potter, Thanos A. Johnson   65

Chapter 11 – Ancestor Newspapers   71

Chapter 12 – Eventful Winters Past – Up the Crystal   79

Chapter 13 – Heartbreak Hotel-Crystal Valley Manor   85

Chapter 14 – An Angel from Heaven -Bleu Stroud   93

Chapter 15 – Shirley and David Thomson   101

Chapter 16 - Chair Mountain Stables   109

Chapter 17 - Marble Community Church   115

Chapter 18 - Marble Charter School   121

Chapter 19 - Hunting in the High Country   129

Chapter 20 –The Thompsons-125 Years in the Crystal Valley   137

Index   145

ACKNOWLEDGMENTS

For such a short word—Book— I have learned 'tis a long linking of people and events to bring one to completion, even a small one such as this, much more than its deceptively simple four letters. This undertaking begins with giving myself permission to "live the dream" and do what I love. That took awhile!

Preparation for *Memoirs of a River...Up the Crystal* began first with being drawn to this valley, then ways manifesting so that we could stay. That connected with my love of listening to old-timers' stories. It all came together by really living the dream—writing about this most beautiful area. So, my first thanks goes to Creator for the blessings of this life.

Doug Whitney, my significant other, gave *Memoirs* its name and me his steadfast support. The manner to give it the light of day came along with the idea of a monthly column with *Crystal Valley Echo* publisher, Alyssa Ohnmacht. Alyssa gave space for *Memoirs* to grow. Much more than an amazing publisher, Alyssa designed this book and kept the project on track. Alyssa is Awesome personified.

Thank you to Carrie Click who taught me a lot about finetuning my writing.

Caleb Begly of *Crystal River Computers* got my website, marbledweller.com, up and running on the mighty complex World Wide Web. He is younger than most of my tee shirts, and just as comfortable to work with, yet very professional. My most grateful thanks to Caleb.

One picture is worth a thousand words; making this book ten pounds lighter. I thank the following photographers and authors who shared their photographic treasures: Rob Hunker and his website, www.ColoradoAerialViews.com;

Meredith Ogilby (photo of Bleu Stroud) from her book, *Women of the Roaring Fork*; Oscar McCollum, Jr. for photos from his two volumes of *Marble: A Town Built on Dreams,*" Dell McCoy for photos from *"Crystal River Pictorial,"* and the Denver Public Library, Western History Department for illustrations and photos in Chapter 1.

Speaking of photos, Serendipity played a part in the front cover photo. This Model A Ford, named Nelly Belle by current owner Gene Hill of Marble, happened to be in front of me one day on the way home to Marble. Gene said that it was manufactured the summer of '29 and had belonged to another long-time Valley resident, Grace Cowen. Folks around here will recognize the name from the Cowen Center in Carbondale. My thanks to Gene for tootling up the road that day in Nelly Belle. Bonus: I look forward to sharing stories about Grace's life and legacy.

You can't learn much about the history of a place, people and the area unless there is a museum and/or historical society nearby. I thank the dedicated volunteers who provided assistance, directions, introductions and materials at the Redstone Historical Society in Redstone, Mount Sopris Historical Society in Carbondale and the Frontier Historical Society and Museum in Glenwood Springs.

Special mention goes to my primary sponsor, the Crystal River Heritage Association (CRHA) in Marble. Knowing my longtime desire to honor the elders of this land, these dedicated history lovers pledged a monthly sponsorship to the early *Echo* for the *Memoirs* column. For more than two years, they honored their Mission Statement to "preserve the unique heritage of the Crystal Valley" by their support of my efforts and growth of the *Echo*. My appreciation many times over to CRHA members and the Board of Directors.

My deepest thanks goes to those folks who shared herein their stories and memories of this very special place. You will enjoy meeting them as much as I have. I am honored that Clifford Duncan, Northern Ute elder, has shared some of the First People's memories and perspectives when this was their homeland.

And to you dear readers who gave me the feedback and encouragement to keep writing, thank you!

Charlotte Graham

Introduction

Dear Reader,

There's an undefined familiarity about this part of Colorado that has certainly captured my heart. You too? Ever since my first day in the Crystal River Valley more than a dozen years ago, I was compelled to learn more about this land. Good thing, because my feet wouldn't leave Marble. True story! Wherever I would walk, intense vibrations would go from the top of my head though my feet into the earth, as though I were connecting to this country like hungry roots of a wildflower.

It all began when artist Doug Whitney, my S.O. (significant other), received an invitation to participate in a weekend Fourth of July art show in the town of Marble in 1997. It turned into a whole summer of mountain discoveries up here for us, including the birth of decade-long friendships. There was such a strong sense of "something" about this place that I was determined to seek out the community's elders, to ask about their youth and ancestors here. Their collective advice: "Don't get involved in Marble politics." Of course, like gum finds a shoe, I waltzed right into a snarly political hornet's nest…more about that in Chapter Eleven.

Leave it be said…we just couldn't leave. All we could think was, how could we hibernate a winter up here? Doug and I turned our landlord's seasonal art gallery into a tiny coffee bar in the old Sneezeweeds building (now residential rental units) located on the north side as one enters town. Folks came in for steaming lattes, Marble baker Joyce Waite's fresh sweet rolls and all the newspapers delivered daily. A real treat for the *New York Times—Wall Street Journal* guys. We organized sleigh rides and art classes, drumming sessions and children's events, and somehow managed to stay afloat and warm. We heard plenty of versions of the Crystal River Valley's history and had a great time with the few winter tourists—mostly lost. *But MapQuest said I could get to Crested Butte from here.*

Between barista duties and outdoor mountain adventures via snowshoe and ski, I had plenty of quiet time that first winter up here to read…and read I did: every page printed, from burnished 1900s newspapers to fifties-style booklets

1

to beautiful four-color, hardbound volumes from thirty years ago. The earliest records, of course, all began with the early white miners and settlers who provided the first written documentation of human life here.

BEAUTY IN THE EYE OF THE BEHOLDER

The more Doug and I learned about this scenic crystalline valley, the more we were smitten…especially with its eccentric community of Marble…long considered the orphaned stepchild of Gunnison County. Or should it have been Pitkin County? After all, we are isolated from, but flanked by, two glamorous step-sisters. On either side of this Snowmass/Elk Mountain range are Aspen in Pitkin County and Crested Butte in Gunnison.

Today, Marble is mostly a residential enclave, a church and school, with a few summer businesses: a general store, RV park, art galleries, and Jeep tours. "Glam" it's not. Gorgeous it is. The further one ventures up Crystal Valley, the less conformed the path. "Wild Child" would more likely describe the upper valley—and its still independent, willful residents. For us, nature beckons, not convenience.

WHO CALLED THIS MEETING? YOU DID!

We started this armchair odyssey, i.e. this book, as a monthly column by the same name in *The Crystal Valley Echo* newspaper in February 2007. It is my effort to honor the memories of those who have lived here before us. As I went along, readers kept suggesting I publish a collection of these monthly features…ergo!

Some of the stories herein are from folks who have lived here for generations; others come from people I've met who return seasonally, annually, or once in a blue moon. Yet all share their own compelling connection to this special place in Colorado. Thirty-year residents have told me, "I didn't know that!" after reading one *Memoirs* story or another. Notably, the stories have delved into many amazing coincidences among us. Gee, do we hear the theme songs of the "Twilight Zone" mixed with "Rocky Mountain High" in the background?

SO THEN, WHAT'S ALL THIS TALK ABOUT A CURSE?

This collection in your hands has a chapter not previously published in the *Memoir* columns of 2007 and 2008.

When this writer read all the available history from the 1880s onward, I found very little information about the first folks who lived in this specific area, even though there were certainly enough stories floating around about the so-called Ute Curse.

"No white man will prosper in this valley," one local told me. "Yeah, it was for a hundred years, but I think they extended it," said another. All versions ended with, "…they cursed the valley and set it on fire on the way out."

Why would the Utes want to do that? Of course, I had to find out more.

WHERE'S THE CONNECTION?

My quest to know more about and honor the Utes, called the *Nuche* (or First People) up here, led me to Clifford Duncan, a Northern Ute elder, living on a reservation in Ft. Duchesne, Utah, due west of Rangely, Colorado. Clifford leads the Ute traditional rituals and ceremonies in their native language, as did his father, Ivan, Grandfather Willie, and Great Grandfather John Duncan. Clifford touches both sides; Indian and non-Indian, by communicating his views of traditional native values and teachings in general public discourse. His desire is to preserve those teachings to both assimilated Utes and whites alike.

One example of Clifford's efforts is to share the less-told story of the Meeker "incident." One hundred thirty years ago, some Utes killed Indian Agent Nathan Meeker after disagreements over the distribution of food supplies being held back. Meeker's death became the basis for the slogan, "The Utes Must GO!" which eventually drove the Northern Utes from Colorado. In 2008, Clifford led the first Ute powwow in Meeker, Colorado since the incident. It was considered by all the participants, Meeker residents and Utes alike, as a time of healing.

Today, Clifford says to those of us who live here, "We are related, you and I. My people lived here for a long time. Now your people live here. We can't change the past, but we have something in common."

He calls that the "original way of thinking," that is, to live communally with nature. It was the Utes' way, encoded in their d.n.a. for hundreds, nay, thousands of years. Clifford's people lived, loved and birthed their children in this Crystal River Valley. "Our spirit here is not dead. It's just been asleep," he says.

TIME TO WAKE UP?

Perhaps it is awakening again. I have met so many who love this valley with all their hearts. Even with different viewpoints and different perspectives, all are to be heard, all are to be honored and all are to be respected. Especially those perspectives handed down with the wisdom of our collective elders. To them we are grateful and can learn much.

Come along on this educational and entertaining journey up and down the Crystal River. We begin with stories from Clifford Duncan, a fourth generation Ute who shares lifeways of his people up here *'way back when* ... and end with Lew Ron Thompson, a fourth generation pioneer who still lives in the house in Carbondale where he was born. His ancestors were the very first settlers when this land became the State of Colorado. Even though they had no way of knowing about each other, Clifford and Lew Ron both said basically the same words to me when approached about their stories in this collection. *We need to know where we came from to know who we are and where we are going.*

For me, story-telling is best when the beginning and ending come around full circle. Between a fourth generation Ute and a fourth generation pioneer settler, this one is complete. I am honored and blessed to present to you, Dear Reader, Volume 1 of *Memoirs of a River-Up the Crystal.*

God Bless this land and all its relations. Aho,
Charlotte Graham
Marble, Colorado, 2009

3

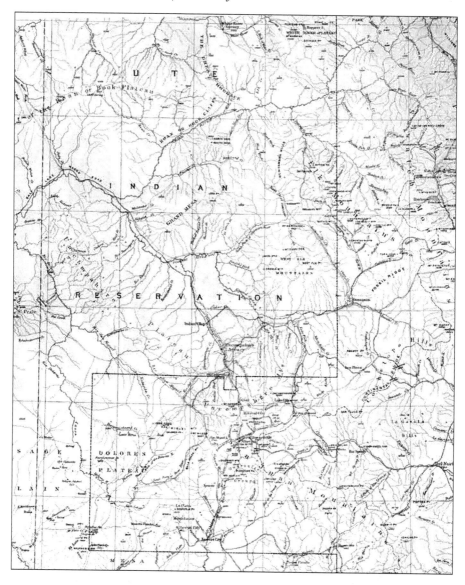

The Original Hayden Map, circa 1877 that defined the Ute Indian Reservation lands "as long as the rivers flow and the grasses might grow." The Elk Mountain range is most specific to the Crystal River Valley today. With even the detailed quarter section, this original map is difficult to read specific areas. Courtesy of Denver Public Library Western History Collection, "Original Hayden Map, 1881," call number cg4311 1881.

Chapter 1

FIRST PEOPLE IN THE CRYSTAL RIVER VALLEY

The Yampatika and Tabewache bands of the Ute Indians were seasonal homesteaders for more than a thousand documented years in western Colorado's mountains. The areas had different names then. We now call them Montrose and Meeker, Leadville, Glenwood Springs, Aspen and Crested Butte. (see map on facing page)

How was life back then? Take in a breath of sweet mountain air and close your eyes.

PUH—NIT—NE
...is a Ute word for "Open your eyes." Exhale. Imagine the Crystal River Valley as your ancestral home. All that is around you are your relations. The birds. The animals. The trees. The sky. Above. Below. To the East. South. West and North. Life was a circle that included all creation equally.

Ute family bands or groups were usually small. "The Utes were on foot; it took a long time to go from place to place," Clifford Duncan, Northern Ute elder said. "They moved around faster, easier after we got horses from the Spaniards."

Come autumn, Ute families would pack up and travel south and west to what is called today the Four Corners area of Colorado, New Mexico, Arizona and Utah. There, they met up with their distant relations, including the Aztecas from southern Mexico and Central America, to enjoy Father Sun's warmth.

They traded and socialized, communicating in what became known to anglo linguistic scholars as the Uto-Aztecan language.

LIVING LARGE

Until around the mid-1800s in the Crystal Valley, Mother Earth was the provider for all her relations, including the Two-Leggeds. She served up a largely rich, relaxing lifestyle in these snowcapped mountains and fertile valleys, where pure, cool, clean mountain waters fed, and her abundant natural hot springs healed all her children. The Utes believed they were closest to Creator when in the high mountains.

Clifford explains that the Utes learned to live in harmony with each other by watching nature. "When Nature completely controls, it will also provide you with every means to survive. Nature is closer to God," he says.

"Nature can take the place of a teacher in a regular school setting. It does not teach you, but opens your eyes to see. For example, you sleep during the night. What makes you get up is the light that hits you in the face. Nobody is there to say get up. It's all in a given time. You get up. You eat. You know you need shelter. Nature provides guidance. Nature is a disciple of Creator. It works for God. God does not work by Itself. It has many providers and Nature is her main teacher. God is first, second is Nature, then Man. God created you. Nature teaches you. Then you become what you are." says Clifford. "That's how I see it."

Thus, from the Utes' perspective, all was well in these mountains—until one certain day in the 1870s when white surveyors first pressed in from the East.

To this valley they came; from over what became the Crested Butte side of the mountains into the future towns of Gothic, Crystal City and on down into Marble. By the dark of one day's sunset, the "longtime locals" knew Change had come to their world.

ONE MAN'S "RICHES" NOT THE OTHER'S

"The first impression of the white people by the observing Indian was, 'Why do you tear it up? That's my Mother Earth,'" Clifford says. They couldn't understand why miners scratched gouges in the earth, clear-cut trees, dynamited holes, poisoned creeks and rivers, and even killed one another looking for certain rocks and minerals they called "silver" and "gold." Even more confusing to the native people, all this decimation was called "riches" by the newcomer.

"That Indian was basing his viewpoint on the fact that the Earth gave him life. Nature provided him the closeness of God. When a man tears up another person's altar, you are naturally going to say, 'That's not right.' And you are going to fight that." Clifford explains. "Nature is a picture of God and that is what the Utes were defending."

UTE WORD FOR "LIVING GREEN"

The Utes lived so lightly on this land, they created the concept of ecology long before that English word was birthed. Thus, evidence of their hundreds of years of habitation were reclaimed by Nature with relative ease. Because they migrated out of the mountains during the winter, in the minds of the newcomers, this rich, beautiful land was here for the taking. Soon, the Ute homeland was declared "uninhabited." Family clans were suddenly no longer free to roam between their summer and winter camps.

In 1880, after the Meeker incident mentioned in our introduction, Utes were corralled at military gunpoint and forced to march some hundreds of miles to a reservation at Ft. Duchesne, Utah. Knee-high granddaughters of that time, who became great-grandmothers themselves, would eventually lose the scent and memory of rain-freshened mountain sage.

For the First People, not only the way of life, but the words of their white brothers were hard to reconcile with their actions. What the Indian saw was inexplicable, devastating actions with little regard for all other of God's creatures. This was to be the way for a long time in the circle of life between native and transplanted Americans. Somewhere along the way, this disconnect from God as Utes understood it eventually led to a civilization lost; by broken promises, broken treaties, and broken traditions of a once-rich social and spiritual life.

Great Grandfather John Duncan (left) led Ute ceremonies in their traditional language during the early 1930s as does his great grandson, Clifford (right) today when visiting the Crystal Valley, April 2008. Left, courtesy of Denver Public Library Western History Collection, "John Duncan in dancing costume," call number X-30466, right, photo by author.

Beneath an article about the Ute "Wars" in Harper's Weekly magazine, October 25, 1879, artist W.A. Rogers caught the gist of how the Utes felt about miners cutting into their Mother Earth for "riches." Courtesy of Denver Public Library Western History Collection, "Prospecting on the Ute Reservation, an ominous meeting," call number Z-4087

LET'S LIVE ANOTHER WAY—WORK, WORK, WORK

By the early 1900s, in the Roaring Fork and Crystal River valleys, most of the silver and other mineral mines went boom and bust. Ghostly remnants of abandoned mining towns were of brick and mortar, log and pitch, not so easily reclaimed by Mother Nature. *Somebody's been here, all right.*

Tenacious Europeans and citizens from Civil War-torn states, all incredibly hardy, found ways to stay up here year-round by developing other ways besides mining to scratch out a living. Through these quiet and more like desperate years, families either dug in or moved on. By the nineteen thirties and forties, new life was breathed back into these abandoned towns, buildings and homes. The settlers worked hard to make better lives for themselves and their families, no matter how difficult the economies of the day. This wealth-deprived era gave birth to a new breed of native sons and daughters in the Crystal River valley region.

Some built up cattle and sheep herds, ranches and farms. Arguably, as rooted people of the earth themselves, theirs was more of a struggle in order to enjoy a dedicated, strongly spiritual life in this land they too loved and revered.

"Ironic," pioneer rancher Lew Ron Thompson said, "We're the same—the Utes and us. We've all been forced off this land, basically for the money."

IF YOU CAN'T BE WITH THE LAND YOU LOVE, LOVE THE LAND YOU'RE WITH

Even though its but a four-hour car trip nowadays from the reservation, Clifford says that since the last four or five generations never knew this area, the Utes of today have no living memory or connection to these mountains, their ancestral homeland.

"They are happy where they live because that is what they know." However, Clifford goes on to say that the mountains play an important role in the reverence to God. "Moses, in the Bible, went to the mountains to speak to God. God spoke to Moses there. This is how the Utes felt close to God. Then the Utes were removed from their mountains.

"They were told to leave their god and their way of living for another, more 'civilized' way. A much different way.

"For the past one hundred thirty years, God's face has been changed. The image of God has been changed. We were told that 'God' looks like this, or this or this…but the mountains look the same, they didn't change. The Sun didn't change. God [as we understand] didn't change."

SO WHERE IS THE CONNECTION?

Clifford says, "It is as though I'm afraid to let go of this one concept of God, because I have been taught to think 'This' is God. I was told to put away my [traditional] ways when I was sent to the white man's boarding schools at age five."

Clifford raises the eternal question facing the Ute people of today. "Who was God to the Ute person of 1880? And who is God to the Ute person of today?"

The Utah reservation where Clifford lives is their home now. Much like jail-born babies, they are content to live their lives within their immediate surroundings, not knowing where their great-grandparents once played as children every summer. Even though the spirit or energy of their ancestors has never left the Crystal River Valley, their descendents most likely will never know what so many of us remark as "something special" about this valley.

"Perhaps the journey of the Native American is to retrace our steps backwards," Clifford says, "to find the true image of what our ancestors knew as God."

"NANAMA," ANOTHER REALLY COOL UTE WORD

Clifford says that in the Ute language, there's a word that phonetically sounds like "Na NA ma." When translated from Ute to English, it means "all together as One." All is the same: Creator, Nature, Human. *Nanama.* "We have to look for that again." he says.

From Christopher Columbus on, he explains, the Indian people became victims. They walked from the light of innocence into the dark experience of exploitation.

"When somebody comes to your home and tells you to get out, you are rejected," he said. "To you, your understanding or meaning is far different than their reason for doing it. You start over here, you know who you are, what you have on [traditional apparel]. And then they tell you to take that off and put this [business suit] on. We don't know what that is."

Clifford says there was a convoluted but concerted effort to strip the Indian from their God, their identity, their way of life. "Over here, you hunt, you gather berries, you follow Nature," he says. "On the other side, [they tell you] to farm. [They tell you], tear up the earth, put corn seed in the ground, potatoes or whatever. Then they square off the land and someone says, 'You live here now, here's [a piece of paper] called a title. Once the white man 'gives' you this land, he takes all of this other land you have always lived on. He says, 'you have this now, you don't need this other land over here.'"

Today, even on the reservation, Clifford says putting up a teepee requires a building permit. "You have to be an 'authority' to build something. Now you have to get a permit to make a fire to have a sweat ceremony in your own backyard." Clifford grins and rubs his forehead vigorously. "What happened?"

"THIS" WAY OR NATURE'S WAY?

There are folks who say, "Life goes on, get over it," or "I can't do anything about what happened in the past." Granted, none of us today can change what happened long ago. But we can, and we do learn from the past. How we can see things in a different way today from the lessons of the past helps us all. Especially when it comes to today's caretaking responsibilities of this special valley we all love. Which is more important now, our way or Mother's way?

Clifford always ends his observations with, "That's what I think, Charlotte. What do you think?" It is obvious that his perspective does not mean to imply a sense of entitlement or an extended hundred year "curse" upon the people who live in the Crystal Valley today. Those times are over. His thoughts are but to shed light and acknowledge the lives, voices and viewpoint of the ancient *Nuche*, the First People of this valley from one of the very last traditional Northern Ute elders. Because, no matter our opinions, after all is said and done, as Clifford says...

"It is up to you now how you take care of this land."

Chapter 2

REDSTONE'S GENERAL STORE

If Redstone is known as the Ruby of the Rockies—which it is—the Redstone General Store should be considered the eighteen-carat gold clasp. It's the only open-year-round general store for twenty-some miles in any direction. And, hey, what's a good story-telling travel adventure without provisions, right?

A REAL K.O.A.

Until the late 1800s, the Ute Indians were sure to camp along the flat land where the General Store sits today. It is easy to imagine their backs to the red cliffs, wide, shallow waters before them. Provisions of the day were plentiful albeit a bit more of a "do-it-yourself" buffet: fish, deer, elk, chokecherries, rose-hips. Shade. Plenty of grass for the horses.

With centuries of habitation under their belts, the Utes were way ahead of us, thinking about warmer places in the dead of winter. They were the first "snowbirds." Come fall, they were outta here. But what do we do?

"NOTHIN' HONEY, JUST SITTIN' ON THE PORCH...."

The first reference to a year-round general store in Redstone comes up when John Osgood, the founder of Redstone, opened the Colorado Fuel and Iron (CFI) company store. During the coal-mining heydays of early 1900s, that store took

"Jack" McClaran, cap in hand, middle, bottom step, circa 1934, was remembered as the friendly fella who first sold bait and beer from their (and Redstone's future general store) porch. He is surrounded by wife, brother, son, cousins and daughter sitting on ground next to horses. Photo courtesy of McClaran collection.

care of supplying provisions for Osgood's miners and their families. That building today has evolved into the Redstone Country Store, a home décor shop owned by Debbie and Bob McCormick.

As for the present-day store, the earliest referenced date I can find goes back to the 1950s when it was owned by O.R. White. Prior to that, stories are told that the house became a store circa 1934 when a friendly sorta fella, "Jack" McClaran, sat on his front porch, a cooler of beer on one side, a cooler of worms on the other. A-w-w-w-w—life was so simple then, eh?

More recent history is a bit easier to find, starting in the 1970s.

HOW HARD COULD IT BE?

Sarah and Martha Herpel are sisters who bought the general store in January 1977 from Charlie and Billie Sue Kerns of Texas. Originally from Florida, the girls went to school in Boulder, migrating over Independence Pass on their outings. One time, they stopped in Carbondale and saw the sales listing for the store. Next thing they knew...the 22 and 24-year-old sisters were selling sausage snacks and six-packs to long lines of black-faced coalminers from the nearby Mid-Continent mine from 8 o'clock in the morning until 8 o'clock at night, seven days a week.

"We lived in the back room so we would work all day, go to bed, get up and open the store," Sarah said. "With maybe a hundred or hundred and twenty people in all of Redstone, the town was really, really, **really** close. We took care of each other, no matter what."

Besides miners, the Herpels catered to campers. Along with fishing equipment, the girls carried the basics: beer, bread and milk. Sarah told how they would break down huge packages of picnic supplies and charcoal and turn them into one-time usage packets for day hikers and one-night campers.

First-aid supplies were well stocked as there were many times when coalminers and cowboys from area ranches got into fights. Sarah remembered how Redstone folks reacted when a man jumped onto the stage of a wedding celebration, waving a .357-magnum pistol at the dancing crowd. Locals leapt on him and held him until Aspen police arrived. Back then, that could take a couple hours, depending on the weather. What am I saying? It still takes that long!

At the mention of weather, Sarah especially remembered the winters. "Redstone was pretty desolate during the winter after the mine shut down. From the Redstone Inn on down the Boulevard, we'd literally be the only light on."

AMERICA'S MOST WANTED...ON THE BOULEVARD?

"We did have one scary time," Sarah admitted. "[serial killer] Ted Bundy had escaped from the Aspen jail. 'Wanted' posters were out on the bulletin board. Here we were—two girls alone in the whole town and a killer on the loose."

All of us who have seen the snow-covered Redstone Inn on a blizzardy night get goosebumps; we are reminded of the similarity of the hotels—the Inn and another Colorado hotel in the movie, "The Shining," made famous by Jack Nicholson.

"H--E-E-E-R-E'S TEDDY!"

One night, Sarah and Martha were closing up the store after a long day of zero business. Suddenly, the blurred lights of a car materialized through the dark, snowy night—they knew no other locals were in town. What if it was Bundy? Or more likely, a lost traveler who needed gas? Should they open the door...or not?

During the decade of the Herpel sisters' ownership, Sarah's husband Gary McClure built the General Store addition. A gas pump is the prominent new feature of the day. Courtesy of Redstone Historical Society.

Twenty-some curvy miles to the next convenience store, a stranded, unprepared person could perish in this cold. As a matter of fact, one person had died recently, the girls knew. The two young women had a lot to consider in less than a minute as the vehicle crept into the driveway...thankfully, it wasn't Ted.

HER INDIAN NAME IS "OUTLASTS THEM ALL"

Who better to talk to than the General Store's longest-time employee (so far), Joyce Illian.

A Marble resident and jewelry designer, Joyce has worked through four of the owners over sixteen years of the store's evolution.

One afternoon, I squatted between the heat stove and fruit stand, sharing the middle of the tiny store with head-high stacks of new deliveries. I looked around. Where to put anything else? This warm, cozy mercantile is no sterilized red and green corporate template; it is an authentic, old-time general store that has it all...with a twenty-first century twist or two.

Joyce shuffled through boxes and filled shelves as she described the store when she first came.

"The packaged-liquor side of the store was the busiest," she said. "That's why we have two separate entrances to the store...state law. I'd come to work at 7 a.m. and there would be a line of cars clear back to the Redstone Inn, as a shift let out from the mine. Men would get their beer on one side and cross over for chips and snacks on the other."

Then coalminer, now real estate agent and long-time denizen Jeff Bier came in for a cup of coffee. He corroborated Joyce's recollection. "The off-shift miners had a saying. 'We're a pint and a six-pack from Carbondale,'" Jeff said.

Sarah and Martha became good marketing providers. "Our motto was if something was asked for three times, we would get it in the store. Would you believe the most sought-after items were bobby pins?" Sarah asked. "With all the weddings in the area, brides never seem to have enough bobby pins."

Sure enough, it was bound to happen that Sarah would need some bobby pins of her own. Seems a coalminer walked into the store one day, McClure was his name. He had come from Pennsylvania to work the Mid-Continent. *Hello, Sarah. Name's Gary.*

Eventually, Gary built the addition to the general store and the Herpel sisters served the community for more than a decade when they sold the store to Darlene Woodward and Martha Collison, partners from California.

"STOP, EAT, GET GAS"

Martha and Darlene now run the Skyline Kennels in Carbondale. "We owned the store from December 1989 until May 1995," said Martha. "We've owned riverfront property in Redstone since 1981. Every time we stopped in the store we would ask the girls to let us know if they wanted to sell."

"With the Mid-Continent mine shut down, we focused on being part of the community, providing what the local folks needed," Martha said. "It was a

Redstone General Store where worms, liquor and gas are still the most popular features unless you count the early-fifties Chevrolet, is it a '53 or '54? Courtesy of Redstone Historical Society

tough go—with the miners went a lot of business, but the locals were very supportive. We added the kitchen and put in a sit-down counter [in the tiny room that today is stocked with canned and packaged food]. We served hamburgers, pizza take-out **a-n-n-d** delivery, mind you, and that is where I created the Redstone egg muffin." Their "Stop, Eat, and Get Gas" T-shirts were really popular at the time. They brought in movie rentals too.

Martha said their fondest memories were the annual Christmas parties at the store. "We'd put out a huge buffet. The whole town and clear up to Marble—everyone was invited."

NEXT OWNER FLYS (AND FITS) RIGHT IN

In 1995, Stephanie and Robert Huntington bought the store from Martha and Darlene. Not much information there. Then in 1998, Jill Briggs, tour manager for jazz musicians Al Jarreau and David Sandborn, was on the road somewhere in Europe when she saw Realtor Bier's ad on the Web for a Colorado mountain resort general store. Jill was ready for a career and lifestyle change. On her next break from the road, she and her boyfriend (now husband) Michael flew out to take a look.

Jill jumped right into the quirky mountain lifestyle. New, different things started happening at the store. "The store to me was not only a way to provide a service to the town," said Jill, "but also serve as a gathering spot. I geared my products to try to eliminate as many trips to Carbondale as I could for people."

Being new to the area didn't faze Jill a bit. "I loved helping people pick out hiking trails and find things to do," she said. She quickly learned everything she could about her surroundings and what was going on in town so she could be helpful to tourists. She said she always loved it when she heard people say, "Let's meet at the General Store."

"I let UPS leave packages," she said, "I kept the keys to the restroom and museum across the street."

After the costly ordeal of upgrading the gas tanks to current safety standards, Jill took after-hours self-serve to a new level by leaving a gallon of gas on the porch for stranded drivers. She'd come back in the mornings with cash on the can from some very grateful travelers.

THERE WERE BEARS... AND BARES

Throughout its history, the store could be slow some days, but pretty entertaining on others. When I asked Jill what particularly funny and interesting events happened while she was running the store, she asked how much room I had in the book! One particularly hot summer day came immediately to mind.

Jill was in the store when a van pulled up as close to the front door as possible. A bare-chested man yelled out the driver's window, "Bring me an ice cream cone."

Jill didn't miss a beat. "What flavor?"

"Strawberry," the man barked.

It so happened that a local resident, Jane Hornsby, was getting ice cream at the store for her grandchildren and offered to take the cone to the man. If it weren't for the fact that Jane is a tall woman, we wouldn't know today that the man was bare all over.

And speaking of bear all over, Jill and Joyce both had to shoo panhandling bears out of the store several times during the summers of drought that brought the bruins down onto the Boulevard.

THUMBS-UP FROM AL GORE

With Jill's organizational skills as a tour manager and her out-going, friendly manner, she attended a Redstone Community Association meeting one time and came home the unanimously-elected president, a position she held for the six years she owned the store. When asked about her favorite accomplishments, again, Jill didn't hesitate.

"I'm exceptionally proud of getting Pitkin County to come to Redstone for recyclables," she said. We think about exponential cause and effect and how significant was her persistence. Now all Crystal Valley residents bring cans, cardboard and bottles down to Redstone twice a month to recycle instead of having to drive to Basalt, an additional hour's drive away. Jill would make Al Gore proud. She sure makes us proud and appreciative of her perseverance.

JUGGLING NO EASY ACT—EVEN FOR A PRO

The next owner was Alyssa Ohnmacht, a valley local all her life who bought the store from Jill in 2004. Alyssa expanded the organic products, including chocolates, dairy and snacks, and offered more locally-grown produce. She also expanded the pastries and sandwich menu and added an ATM, producing organic greenbacks—just kidding.

Lattes, wraps and gourmet soups hit the scene, relegating Folgers and Dinty Moore to lower shelves…but still available.

Although she loved the store and business, Alyssa had to make a difficult decision early 2007. A single mother of two young daughters, Alyssa's plate was more than full. Besides the girls, she was busy with the store, *The Crystal Valley Echo*—our valley's monthly newspaper, building a house and her many volunteer duties at the Marble Charter School and in the community. And all done well! Whew! But something had to give. Thus it was with regret that she decided to put the Redstone General Store up for sale.

ONE OF THOSE FUN COINCIDENCES

The next owners to step into the never-dull world of retail-in-the-middle-of-nowhere were and still are, Michael and Lisa Schlueter and their daughters, Victoria and Lauren.

Lisa told us that she first came to Marble when she was ten years old, about half way between the ages of her two girls today.

"Dad had been coming up here for twenty-five years." Lisa said, "He'd rent the Williams House. I remember walking from the house with my cousin Andy to the Gold Pan Gallery. It seemed like a long ways back then." Actually, it was just a quarter of a mile distance, still a long way for little feet. "Michael and I met in high school in Tucson," Lisa said. "We've lived there all our lives. I brought him up here and he fell in love with the area too."

What we find out next is a perfect example of the incredible coincidences that happen in the Crystal River Valley.

About the time Alyssa was counting the number of balls she had in the air and what to do about them all, Lisa and Michael decided to get a summer cabin in Marble. They found the perfect home, one of the most remote houses in the upper Crystal Valley…at the top of Daniels Hill.

Michael piped in. "It [the house] came with a snowcat, snowmobile and ATV, if that is any indication of what we were getting ourselves into. We didn't care, it was a 'summer' place we said…" He winked. "…R-r-right!"

Nevertheless, daughters Victoria and Lauren loved their new home, never complaining about the hard realities of living on a remote mountain hillside. When they left that fall to return to Tucson, Lisa said that she and the girls cried all the way up and over McClure Pass. "We were heartbroken." Lisa said. "We didn't want to leave."

MOUNTAIN-SIZED ECHO REACHES THE DESERT

They were very smart people, Michael and Lisa. Why? Before they headed back home, they subscribed to *The Crystal Valley Echo*. I'm not saying here that lottos are won, miracles happen, or anything like that when folks subscribe to the *Echo*, but….

The following April, Alyssa listed the Redstone General Store with Jeff Bier.

An eye-catching, four-color glossy of the store was in his real estate advertisement.

"When I saw that, I couldn't believe it!" Lisa said. "We could live in Marble, have a business in Redstone, the girls could go to the [Marble] Charter School. It was the perfect opportunity. I showed Michael the ad and we called Jeff."

Like climbing Mount Everest, they both gloss over what it took for them to accomplish, but here they are now, bright, smiling faces in the store, planning out their own expansion plans. They started by adding more than seventy-five tons of dirt to the store's backyard, creating a cool retreat with a wishing well, and fun things to do for the children, like a gold-panning sluice, a mini-town play area and huge logs for seating around a campfire.

Lisa said they have lots of ideas, more than they can do all at once so there's much to look forward to at the store. One change I noticed, all the beverages in the cooler are oddly priced: $1.62, $.84, $2.37. "It's my way of saving pennies," Lisa said, laughing. "With tax, the total on one-item sales comes out to an even amount."

ALL BUT 31 FLAVORS—THANK GOODNESS

All Redstone General Store owners agreed on one thing: No question—the community, up and down the valley, supports the store, and so do the tourists who flock during summer season. "I hand-dipped 400 cones in one day over Fourth of July," exclaimed Michael, "to the point that my arm muscles cramped up."

Each owner has brought their labors and signature additions to the store. And, as Joyce Illian noted before she finally retired in 2007, the previous owners have always helped the next owner.

The store still serves as the local news headquarters…if anything happens in the community, good or bad, folks come to the store to find out. With a half-century of commercial history, it appears the Redstone General Store is poised for yet another exciting chapter with Michael, Lisa, Victoria and Lauren Schlueter.

Okay, folks, time to grab up your favorite snacks and move on down the road. For a couple, maybe three Washingtons, you can grab a bar of Dagoba organic dark chocolate with lavender and blueberries or how about a handful of (still) penny candy like Bit-O-Honey or Tootsie Rolls?

Chapter 3

FILOHA MEADOWS

Now, before we get ready to shove off to our next adventure—did I mention that many a time a story is just that—a story!¿ I try most diligently to get facts straight, but sometimes lore and legend, such as the romanticized "Ute Curse" have become improvable gospel—or in some cases, pure guff. I've discovered that sometimes details of the same names, dates and places can vary, but in any case, save your hangin' rope for a potted plant. I present these stories as just that—stories—of life-gone-by in this very special place, the Crystal River Valley.

We're headed a couple miles downriver of the Redstone General Store, to the base of Mount Sopris, where geothermal springs bubble up throughout a three-mile alpine meadow. The entire valley is known today as Filoha Meadows. Chair Mountain reigns to the south.

This remarkable ecosystem was known in post-Ute days as (one of many) Hot Springs, Colorado. The area is home to an exotic array of flora and fauna. This ecosystem is unusual in the high country for rare orchids, fireflies, big-eared bats, and mooning...I mean calving...elk and bighorn sheep. I'll explain the mooning later.

As for the two-legged population; for hundreds of years and then after a poetic treaty or two by the white man that used the following as a timeline, "as

"A fine guest house with dining facilities was built close to the track, while a bath house was right down next to the river" reads the description of the Penny Hot Springs Inn circa 1935 in Dell McCoy's publication, "The Crystal River Pictorial. " Courtesy of Sundance Publications Ltd.

long as the rivers run and as grasses might grow," the Ute Indians thought theirs was the rightful stewardship of this land. A few pieces of paper known as the Brunot peace treaty changed that in 1873.

During the next decade or so, after the Utes were expelled in 1880, miners pecked for lead, zinc and other minerals up and around the shanks of Mount Sopris. Evidently they found more financially viable veins of silver and such in the hillsides of Aspen and Leadville, leaving behind recalcitrant mines on this side full of nothing but busted efforts.

WANNA KNOW HOW TO MAKE A LAWYER CRY?

Homesteading was how land was acquired up into the early twentieth century. Without benefit of time or primo eyesight to scan through early Pitkin County microfische records for confirmation, it was fun to pull on the spaghetti strands all mixed together of early ownership memories and chat with various elders today, telling about this particular area. Whilst I'd love to share all of the stories I heard while learning about Filoha Meadows, I'll stick to visits with some of the owners going back to the 1940s and on...even if one of the stories involved one man saying, "If you throw in a horse, it's a deal." With the exchange of a bridle, attached to a horse, *lots* of land between Filoha Meadows and Snowmass changed hands. Didn't need hundreds of notarized pages to know who they were and what they wanted. Hummm...a major land swap consummated with a horse and a handshake...or a few pounds of legal documents? Let's go on...don't want to make the lawyers cry.

Lush Italian gardens of
Kelly and Linda Grange at
Hot Springs Ranch, adjacent
to Penny Hot Springs.
Famous Redstone artist,
Jack Roberts often sketched
Linda's blossoms to include in
his paintings. Courtesy of
Grange collection

VALLE d'AOSTA—MEET YOUR YOUNGER VALLE

Joseph Grange was a rancher and farmer during the forties who pastured his cattle at Hot Springs, moving them up to Lily Lake near Marble in the summers. The land he owned has been kept in his family for some fifty years. I got to chat with son, Kelly and his wife, Linda, who now live in Grand Junction, Colorado.

In the early 1900s, the Granges were part of a large Italian immigration to the Roaring Fork Valley that came to work the silver and coal mines around Aspen. Many families came from little villages in and around Valle d'Aosta on the Italian/French border. They must have felt like they had come home when they arrived—from the most beautiful mountains in the Alps to the most beautiful mountains in the Rockies.

VIVA LA DOLCE VIDA

Italians brought with their Catholic heritage a love of food and wine and a knack for high-altitude gardening. It's been said that one could drive through Carbondale and pick out which were the Italian gardens! Kelly and Linda were reputed to have traffic-stopping gardens at their Hot Springs Ranch home up the Crystal. People would pull over to admire Linda's rose bushes, marigolds and snapdragons. Jack Roberts, the famous Redstone artist and good friend of Kelly and Linda, loved to come and sketch flowers in their yard and then incorporate them in his paintings.

What Italian could live *la dolce vida* without wine? It wasn't long before every fall, train cars of California grapes would arrive by rail to the Emma train station where young Kelly would go with his dad in a wagon to get the grapes and take them home to make wine. A favorite memory? When Kelly and his playmates slurped on slivers of the ice used for refrigeration all the way home.

Kelly remembered how his dad used to take horses from their ranch in Basalt and walk them upvalley to their Hot Springs ranch where he would use them to plow the field for seed potatoes. At the end of the planting, he'd release the horses. The horses would then wander back downvalley through Carbondale and up to Basalt where Kelly would see them at their feed station in the barn a few days later. For those readers not familiar with the terrain, this is a good fourteen miles to Carbondale and then another twelve or fourteen miles up towards Aspen to Basalt! Brings new appreciation for that bumper sticker, "Not all who wander are lost."

Didn't you worry?

No, not then.

There still barely exist fallen relics of popular therapeutic hot springs bathhouses from the thirties dotting the meadow and riverside. "The Crystal River Pictorial" by Dell McCoy shows a picture of Penny Inn, in the middle of the meadow, featuring the earliest known "spa dining" facilities with separate bath houses for men and women down by the river. Penny was the namesake caretaker of that property. It was quite the social event to board a train from Carbondale to take the waters and enjoy the unparalleled scenery. Of course, there were proper separate bath houses for the men and women.

WE'RE IN SOME HOT WATER NOW!

Today, that which people call Penny Hot Springs next to Highway 133 is actually Granite Springs, according to a current neighbor and former owner of Filoha Meadows, Dr. Bernarr Johnson, a retired orthopedic surgeon at Loma Linda Hospital in California. "Penny Springs is still out in the middle of the meadow," he told me. In fact, I learned that Filoha is full of bubbling hot springs.

Bernarr and his bride of sixty-plus years, Dorothy, were gracious hosts to me as we visited about their life here in the Crystal Valley. Dorothy, a former teacher, said, "Filoha Meadows was named after a hospital we served in Ethiopia during the fifties when my husband was a missionary doctor there. Filoha means 'hot water' ['fil woha' in Amharic] and the hospital was nicknamed that because of a hot spring that came up there."

The Johnsons found there were already several names for the many hot springs that gurgled up all around them: not only was there Penny Springs, but Hot Springs, Firefly Springs, and the aforementioned Granite Springs throughout Filoha Meadows. Bernarr wanted to name the property Firefly Meadow but Dorothy's choice prevailed. "She always wins!" Bernarr joked.

Bernarr and Dorothy had looked at many hot spring properties in Colorado after they retired because they wanted to have small retreats to cater to patients with rheumatoid arthritis. Mineral baths were proven beneficial in early treatment and preventative care. They built two duplex cabins with small hot pools on the property when they first moved in the early 80s. Since the therapy wasn't covered by insurance, it didn't work out.

Their son-in-law, Alan Nelson, M.D., then used the cabins for awhile for marital counseling for doctors and their wives, similar to the work of his associate, the late Louis McBurney at the Marble Retreat for ministers and their wives. The Marble Retreat is its own story for another time.

Penny (really Granite) Hot Springs on a winter morning. Each summer, the ponds are rebuilt by avid local soakers. Author photo

THE FUTURE'S UNDERFOOT

Those endeavors were second, however, to Bernarr's consuming passion to make use of the geothermals percolating under his feet. "This land is very interesting and beautiful," he said. "There are all kinds of hot water sources here. Interest in geothermal is becoming more important as a renewable energy source."

Bernarr built all kinds of piping to capture the hot water from Penny Springs. "Its temperature is very hot, 130 degrees, compared to [the hot springs in] Glenwood Springs, which is 127 degrees," he explained as he showed me how he laid a quarter mile of pipe from the spring to the Johnsons' house, to a heat exchanger, where clean water is then piped through the house and greenhouse. The water returns to a settling pool at 104 to 106 degrees, keeping rooms in the house at 70 degrees in the coldest weather. The water is then returned to the ponds and then to the river. After years of refinement, Bernarr feels the heat system is good, but could be better yet.

"I'm an expert on pipes...should have been a cardiologist" he mused.

"Yes, there are pipes everywhere!" Dorothy exclaimed.

If that doesn't get your eco-friendly attention, how about this? Bernarr filled their thousand gallon propane tank ten years ago and it is still at 60 percent!

"We only run the standby propane generator about ten minutes a week. We have to make sure if the electricity goes out, the pump doesn't freeze up," said Bernarr.

Dorothy added, "We've had a pile of firewood next to the house for the last twenty years. We don't even need to use a wood stove."

Bernarr believes that it is just a matter of time until the hot waters that flow beneath this valley floor become even more interesting as a renewable energy source for area residents.

"It's been done it in communities in Oregon and Iceland," he said. "Why not here?"

IT'S NOT *ALL* ABOUT YOU, MR. TWO-LEGGED!

Besides the geothermal rarity of Filoha Meadows, if there was such a rating, this area would be a five-star hotel for wildlife and rare species of plants. In 2003, Pitkin County Open Space and Trails purchased nearly two hundred acres around Filoha Meadows. These conservation easements help insure protection of critical habitat found unique to this place.

And what a list it is: Green/white Bog orchids flourish in the summer while what we as kids used to call "lightning bugs" flit about at dusk in the wetland meadows. The rare Little beaked spike rush can be found here. Lynx, extremely rare, have been sited padding quietly across the meadow. Beavers build their own affordable housing with bald eagles and peregrine falcons surveiling their construction from above. Townsend's big-eared bats roost in the steamy warm, dark caves and crevices of the granite hillsides.

"At 6 a.m. one day," Dorothy said, "I looked out at the potato field. Elk had come down and had birthed their calves by the river. It was cute watching the babies bouncing up and down like goats and the trouble those parents had when they started herding them up the hill to a big pasture over the other side. The babies wanted to stay and play."

No kidding, folks, at a seven thousand foot elevation, there are bats, fireflies, orchids, and goldfish—oh, yeah, did I mention the story about how apparently a boy and a girl goldfish mysteriously ended up in one of the ponds, hence today's golden carp population that thrives in the warm waters even when surrounded by snow?

FROM HERE ON OUT—IT'S A TALL TALE

This valley is a high country paradise, unparalleled. No wonder it was the perfect spot in 1993 for a Disney movie called "Tall Tales," starring Patrick Swayze.

A barn was built as a full set, interior and exterior, and had to be torn down after the production was completed. Pitkin County allowed the Johnsons to keep a small portion of the building, which had to be moved to where the greenhouse sits today. The water wheel we see from the road, while not operable, was left behind as well.

Left, Bernarr Johnson, M.D., owner of Filoha Meadows until 2003 purchase by Pitkin County's Open Space and Trails. Faux water wheel (and real green house) behind him can still be seen from Highway 133. Author photo.

Above, set of *Tall Tales* filming in 1993. $10,000 worth of plastic flowers were added to make the meadow more realistic. Wonder how the "locals" felt? Photo by Ron Miller

Ron Miller, a long-time Marble resident, worked for five weeks with the film crew that fall. Ron said, "I was promoted to assistant greensman after I helped build the barn. Besides covering guard rails and telephone poles with camouflage, I had to sprinkle $10,000 worth of plastic flowers in the meadow." Aiding and abetting Mother Nature, Disney-style.

"It was fun but sometimes it could be very boring, waiting for something to happen." Ron said. "I gained ten pounds from all the catered food on the set."

According to Gary Tennenbaum of Pitkin County Open Space and Trails, the county wrote a management plan for the area that was presented to the public in 2007. It is hoped that those plans will continue to accommodate the annual Fireflies & Orchids Walk at Filoha Meadows each summer, sponsored by the Roaring Fork Conservancy.

After the wildlife sightings, probably the most popular attraction at Filoha Meadows is the natural hot spring pools next to Highway 133. For more than thirty years, people have been using Penny Hot Springs, nicknamed at one time the "skinny-dip" springs. At any given time, there can be a half a dozen vehicles pulled over next to the bluff. Come spring, the snow run-off pretty much knocks out the stone-lined pools but devotees build them back up every year.

As for the mooning I spoke of earlier, it's not what you might guess. Directly across the river from Penny [really Granite] springs, is where bighorn sheep and elk winter feed—their pale blond rear ends always pointed at the funny two-leggeds with their clicking boxes.

Chapter 4

BRB—ROCK CREEK SCHOOLHOUSE

If you've traveled on Highway 133 since 1963, besides noticing the ole dirt road turned asphalt, you would have noticed an RV park and campground on the right, half way down from Penny Hot Springs towards Carbondale. Dotting the south end of the river are rustic red cabins, with RV and tent sites towards the north end of the resort.

BRB is a landmark well known by locals; "…go two miles past BRB," or "…remember, your cell phones don't work after BRB," or "…watch out for the mudslide south of BRB."

PULL A NICKEL OUT OF YOUR POCKET

If I had a nickel for every time those three initials were said by folks like me, who haven't the slightest idea what it means, well, I'd have a lot of nickels. Thus, the first words tumbling out of my mouth after introductions with former owner Donna Burkett was "What does BRB mean?"

Stay close, now.

"My husband, Bobby Raymond, was the only child of Raymond and Velma Burkett," Donna said. From the photos she shared, I could see how Donna was smitten with the handsome, dark-haired Airman First Class just returned from service in Tripoli, North Africa in 1961.

"His folks came from Terrell, Texas, in the Dallas area," she said. "Because they loved to camp, hunt and fish, they bought this portion of riverfront land from Bob Sewell, Sr. who owned land across the river and on the west side of 133 in the early sixties."

After she graduated from high school, the Carbondale native and Bobby got married. Before you could say "Honeymoon's over," Donna was enlisted to skin logs for the cabins' construction.

"We were putting the roof on Cabin 14 when Velma ran out and hollered up to us. She had heard on the radio that President Kennedy had been shot," Donna said.

The Burketts' plan was to operate the campground in the summer and leave in the winter, as the Utes had done a hundred years before. But they found that the business of even the most idyllic inclination is still a business; they ended up working year-round to make a living for their families.

They opened BRB Campground and Crystal River Resort in 1963 with six cabins and the main lodge. Every inch of their business card advertised the resort amenities, including a private lake fed by the river at the north end of the property stocked by the fish and game department. The lake has since been drained and reclaimed for tent sites. Four more duplex cabins were added that became year-round rentals when those dam workers came out in 1965 to build the nearby Reudi Reservoir above Basalt.

"We had a bar and a kitchen in the main lodge, maybe three or four tables." Donna said. "We cooked and served meals every day along with cleaning the cabins and campsites."

After Donna and Bobby had their first of four children, they moved back to Carbondale in 1966 where Bobby opened "Bob's Trading Post" in a building that still sits next to the railroad tracks. His folks stayed at BRB until 1972. For twenty-five years, Bob sold gear and guns to eager hunters and fishermen as he shared his Texas-sized experiences of the Crystal River terrain. "Those Texans can sure tell a story," smiled Donna. "I'm familiar with that!"

A SULTAN PITCHES HIS TENT

"I've found the friendliest people in the whole world are from Texas," said current BRB owner, Omar Sultan. He and Ruth, his wife of thirty-some years, bought the property in 1995. They knew the campground well, having come out from California every year since 1973.

Omar talked about the changes at BRB the last four decades as we walked the property's perimeter.

What is left besides Gloria Taylor's vivid memories, is this log cabin frame that used to be the Rock Creek Schoolhouse. Current BRB owner, Omar Sultan makes every effort to preserve as best he can.

"That's one thing that hasn't changed—families that have been coming here every summer for forty years, mostly from Texas, Oklahoma, Louisiana but also from Denver and the Front Range." remarked Omar. Ruth added, "Many of these folks have become like family to us. It is really sad when they write and say they can't come anymore."

But what *has* changed is significant. And costly. "Probably over six hundred thousand dollars in improvements spent since we came," Omar said. "The first year, we buried the electrical lines underground and then we upgraded the septic. We now have a state-of-the-art thirty-five thousand-gallon system with a flood-proof leach field that cleans waste water to nearly pure again." Anyone thirsty?

MONEY DON'T GROW ON TREES

But one can hope. Omar and Ruth spent seventy or eighty thousand dollars in spruce, pine and aspen trees they planted six years ago. Most are maturing and filling out, creating camper privacy from Highway 133. Where there had been fifty-five camp sites over the years, Omar culled out and created more space between the sites. Today, there are less than forty sites with the original thirteen cabins. "Burketts built those cabins to last," said Omar.

SCHOOL BELLS DON'T RING HERE ANYMORE

We had nearly completed our circle around the grounds when we passed a brown-painted skeleton of a covered wagon sitting next to a graying, roofless structure in front of the main lodge.

"What's this, Omar?"

He led me around to the rear of the old building. Faintly etched into a log sign was "Rock Creek Schoolhouse-1884." We know that Rock Creek was the Crystal River's name 'way back when.

"I don't know much about the school or when it closed," admitted Omar. "I have had folks tell me that it was a polling place for a number of years in the thirties and forties."

While he would like to save the historic old schoolhouse, Omar knows by experience that the expense required of today's engineering and building permit

Top to bottom: Bobby Raymond and father Raymond with their hunting trophies, Grandpa Raymond and Grandma Velma Burkett with Bobby and Donna's first daughter, Missy, Bobby Raymond just a stone's throw from the river with a mess o'trout for supper.

process would far outweigh the sentimentality of saving memories of the past...even as it disintegrates in his front yard.

With a sad heart knowing the inevitable, I peeked inside. A boarded up front door, windows too. The floor was carpeted in grass. I looked up. The sky was the limit. *School bells, school bells*...how does that rhyme go? Could I find anyone today who was in attendance when the old school bell of Rock Creek Schoolhouse rang?

MOBLEY, WHITBECK, TAYLOR...HEAD TO TOE, GLORIA'S NAMES ARE TALLER THAN SHE IS!

Next stop: Carbondale's newly refurbished Mt. Sopris Historical Museum and an introduction to volunteer docent, Linda Criswell. "Know anyone who went to Rock Creek Schoolhouse?" Linda quickly asked a local elder, Mary Lilly, who said, "Talk to Gloria Taylor. She's a Whitbeck."

What a delightful telephonic visit I had with this sharp-minded septuagenarian. Gloria Whitbeck Taylor's family tree has had significant historical notables during their four generations in the Crystal River Valley.

After the Civil War, Gloria's great-grandfather, John Chester Mobley came from Kiowa, Colorado via Crested Butte, over Schofield Pass. He formed a settlement named Clarence below Crystal City in 1880. The town of Clarence might be around today but for the designation that the post office appointment gave to a neighboring mining town called Marble.

Nellie, Mobley's eldest daughter, was Gloria's grandmother...who married a Whitbeck. In 1894-95, the Whitbecks homesteaded their ranch where Nettle Creek empties into the Crystal River at about mile marker 159. Mentions of the Whitbeck road crossing are in the Oscar McCollum book, "Marble, A Town Built on Dreams, Volume 1."

THE BEST SCHOOLIN'

One-room schoolhouses were common from Missouri Heights to Marble, serving the surrounding, and very isolated farming, ranching and mining families. Gloria was born in Glenwood Springs when soon after, the family moved to their home at the base of Mount Sopris. The school was a mile downvalley from the family farm on what we know now as Highway 133. She attended Rock Creek Schoolhouse in the mid-thirties for first and second grades before the school finally closed.

When I described the current condition of the little schoolhouse and the split log sign posted on the back wall's exterior, Gloria said, "Oh, I remember that back wall. That is where the woodstove sat in the corner.

"The teacher was Edna Maley," Gloria went on. "I can remember the other six students the years I was there. There was Clyde Worley, Ruth Worley, Vernon Worley, Ronald Dawson, Maezell Dawson, Lavina Ogden and myself."

Gloria was a tiny bit of a six-year old when she did these one-mile treks through feets of snow by herself those two winters. Every day. Never absent. Never tardy. But for that one day....

"I was near what was then called the old Peterson Place about half way to school. I got really cold." Gloria recalled. In all the old history books of the Crystal Valley, there are stories and photos of how much snow accumulated in the early twentieth century. Even fifty, sixty, seventy years ago, the snow was often five feet high in the flat valley floor. That one day, the barely three-foot child sat down on the side of the snow-enveloped road, unable to move even another inch. "I was so cold," Gloria said.

At the schoolhouse, the seat of the never-absent, never-tardy child was empty. After awhile, Mrs. Maley knew something was wrong. She got in her car and drove up the road until she found the little girl half-hidden in the snow-bank, huddled against the biting cold. Gloria remembered how grateful she was as the teacher bundled her up and carried her back to the school and to the woodstove against that back wall. She sat on her teacher's lap while Mrs. Maley rubbed the child's numbed hands and feet back into circulation.

Back at the ghostly gray ruin of a schoolhouse, you can visualize the scene at that back wall. The nice warm, woodstove over in the corner. A lucky little girl. It's only one of many, many stories contained within the crumbling structure.

BRB Resort and Campground entrance – 2008. Author photo

MOO-VING EXPERIENCE

If winter weren't enough, Gloria remembered other terrifying times when ranchers would herd their cattle up and down the same road spring and fall.

These days, adults, insulated by a temperature-and-odor controlled ton of steel and glass, absolutely freak out when the few remaining cattle are driven through Carbondale between summer and winter pasture. Imagine the pint-sized perspective of a mass of mooing bovines literally bearing down over the top of a little one's head.

It so scared Gloria that her father talked to the herders and after that, whenever the cowboys thought little Gloria might be on the road, they would ride ahead of the herd, and lift Gloria up onto their saddles so she could watch the portly procession from a safe, high perch. Then they'd swing her down again to continue on her way.

Gloria and her daughter Ceri, shared these memories at their Grand Junction home. Perusing old albums and out-of-print books, I left with the certainty that Great-Grandfather Mobley deserves a chapter of his own someday.

Oil paintings of scenery on the Taylor living room walls looked familiar. Gloria told me that her portrait of Mount Sopris was done when she was an art student of another Marble icon, Bleu Stroud. We'll learn more about Bleu soon.

In 2009, the BRB Resort is up for sale. Is another chapter about to be writ? We'll be back someday to find out. Come along; no river waits.

Chapter 5

SATANK

Turning north of BRB, we armchair adventurers find ourselves following the Crystal River past century-old farms and ranchlands, through Carbondale to where the Crystal and Roaring Fork rivers converge. In 1884, there was a townsite here founded by Isaac Cooper and Frederick Childs. This town was named Cooperton, then Rockford, Sutank, Moffat and finally, Satank, when the gentlemen Cooper and Childs filed for a post office.

POSTMARK MAKES THE DIFFERENCE
The name Satank may have come from the Kiowa Chief Satanka, or Sitting Bear. Satanka was recognized at that time as a defiant tribal leader. Research falls short in finding an actual connection between the person, Chief Satanka, and the town so named. There is, however, a recurring stitch that weaves through early Roaring Fork and Crystal River valley towns. Irrespective of the source of their financial lucre or the numbers of schools and saloons, the fates of these mountain towns were really driven by their post offices and train stations. And Politics sat in the front seat.

For instance, the town of Clarence (founded by John C. Mobley of Chapter Four) lost out to across-the-creek Marble due to Marble's founders allegedly having an "in" with Postmaster General John Wanamaker. Satank also lost the toss when Carbondale,

Early undated photo of confluence of Roaring Fork (bottom left) and Crystal River (bottom right). Satank is on the left. Mount Sopris at the top. Courtesy of Colorado Rocky Mountain School

a mere fifty-two-hundred-and-some-feet away, got its post office. So too, went the lobbying for the train station. With both towns building railroad tracks in anticipation, the tracks literally went south when Mr. Cooper died during mid-negotiations with Mr. Moffatt, the main railroad man.

WHERE'S THE LUCK—HERE, HERE OR THERE?

Back then, miners up in Aspen struck it rich. Miners up the Crystal mostly busted out. In today's Crystal City—the two-legged population is zero in the winter and a couple dozen residents in the summer. In twenty-first century Aspen—newspaper headlines blithely announce a real estate sale for two hundred and twenty three million. As in $$$. Even with decades of the Crystal Valley's kinder, gentler development by farmers and ranchers, Carbondale's affordable housing in today's world comes in at more than four hundred thousand, and I don't mean potatoes. Makes you wonder what is really the Curse? While attributed to the Utes, who had no concept of dollars, it seems we're the ones paying the price to be here.

CURSED OR NOT

Numerous Ute artifacts have been found all around Red Mountain at the intersection of Highways 82 and 133 between Carbondale and Glenwood Springs. Epic battles were recorded from the early 1800s. It is not so difficult to imagine how the First People stood in awe of the pristine beauty surrounding the mountain valley plain. Red Mountain stands to the north guarding over verdant green meadows splayed across the base of a snow-wrapped mountain named Sopris to us—We-mu-ya-ca-zus to them.

The Utes' other relations—the winged, the four-legged, the water creatures—eagle, elk, deer and trout; well, their descendents can and still do migrate to this valley floor and waters each spring.

By the late 1880s, even though Isaac Cooper and Frederick Childs built a store to house their post office, a hotel, a saloon and a school, sparking a bit of a boom in Satank, the railroad bypass to Carbondale doomed the fledgling metropolis.

Pagoda-topped CRMS Barn stands out in its field...as do many of its alumni...for innovative use of space and materials; just as cutting edge in 2008 as in 1898 when this building was designed and built. Today, CRMS students lead the way in programs of self-sustainability whether through bio-diesel fuels, solar energy and organic stewardship of the land. Author photo.

BAR FORK RANCH—COLORADO ROCKY MOUNTAIN SCHOOL

Isaac went on to be a significant influence in the development of Glenwood Springs, hence the named Cooper Street. Isaac's daughter, Alice married Nathaniel Hubbard and they built a summer home on the Cooper Ranch in Satank and named it "Bar Fork."

Mt. Sopris Historical Society vice president and Satank resident, Greg Forbes, told me that the Bar Fork changed hands over time until Harold "Shorty" Pabst donated some three hundred and fifty acres of the ranch to Colorado Rocky Mountain School (CRMS) for their campus in the early nineteen fifties. CRMS is a college prep school that focuses not only on academics and sports but is a salient supporter of its community. The founders John and Anne Holden felt that "work breeds confidence, self-satisfaction, the will to live."

CRMS students have become leaders in the stewardship and sustainability of its land and beyond. They began solar energy experiments in the seventies and have programs today in the study and production of bio-diesel fuels. The alpine gardening season kicks off with hardy seedlings for sale each May from the school's organic garden greenhouse. CRMS students extended their steward-ship endeavors for at least two spring breaks by volunteering to help the rebuilding of Pearlington, Mississippi after Hurricane Katrina.

One might wonder about the unusual pagoda-style barn at CRMS seen from Highway 133. It was originally built in 1898 as a hundred by hundred foot square, with a four-sided roof, using an oriental trussing system. It's since been converted into a library, classrooms and a theater.

SATANK REVITALIZATION PLAN—WHAT SHELF IS IT ON?

As Greg Forbes showed me around a bit, he said, "Satank sunk to its lowest

population point sometime in the sixties but little by little in the seventies, people began to move back."

Some folks still live in a few of the original buildings that were updated as residences and prefer their autonomy from city regulations such as streetlights and sidewalks. They don't mind that their roads are less traveled, especially since the closing of the bridge. The Satank Bridge is the longest-spanning wooden truss bridge in Colorado. At a hundred and ten years old, the old bridge was getting a little long in the truss so the Town of Carbondale and Garfield County shut it down to vehicular traffic some years ago. They are working on grant applications for a restoration project and plan the rebuilding soon. As with the Rock Creek Schoolhouse structure, preservation and restoration of historic buildings and sites in today's world are an altruist's domain.

Top: the village of Satank, Colorado in 1885 is the main stagecoach stop before the railroad bypassed them for Carbondale one mile apart. Courtesy of Sundance Publications, *"Crystal River Pictoral."* Bottom: The longest spanning wooden-truss bridge in Colorado, Satank's bridge is in dire need of repair. Author photo

Chapter 6

1881—THE OLD THOMPSON HOMESTEAD

&

THE SUSTAINABLE SETTINGS RANCH—2003

Our next journey up the Crystal transports us with the eyes of the Eagle, the most powerful of the winged relations according to Ute stories. Hang on now as we continue this upstream adventure.

"MR." EAGLE'S GIFT

This ability to glide upvalley on the wings of an eagle is a gift given to our readers by our own "Mr. Eagle," a.k.a. Rob Hunker, Redstone resident, avalanche expert by trade and aerial photographer by passion.

We've done our best to reproduce a color photograph taken by Rob. For readers not versed in the electronic World Wide Web universe, now is the time to "make nice" with a grandkid, niece or nephew with one of those computer contraptions. Have them punch in www.ColoradoAerialViews.com, the homepage of Rob's aerial photography studio. I promise that you will thoroughly enjoy his stunning photography. It is a perspective most of us won't ever have otherwise.

"Eagle-eye" view of north end of Crystal Valley, Carbondale at center top. Highway 133 is the white line bisecting the middle of the photo and Highway 82 is skirting around Red Mountain to the north (top). Photo by Rob Hunker, ColoradoAerialViews.com.

The aerial view in this first photo from Rob is looking north or downvalley. Carbondale is in the upper half. From this perspective, let's assume we are making a landing lower-center and to the left, out in those open fields. This could be bumpy. The ground is coming up pretty fast. Whoa, what's out there in the field? Those long-haired bovines sure aren't cattle or buffalo. Yaks, you say? O-kay, we're getting pretty close...do they bite? *Hey, slow down, Mr. Eagle!*

Five miles south of Carbondale, only a few feet from Highway 133 stands the 1881 homestead cabin and ranch of the one of the very first valley settlers, the Thompson clan. Today, Brook and Rose Le Van of Sustainable Settings Ranch produce foods for locals from this farm: poultry, meat, eggs and vegetables. Brook said that Sustainable Settings is not only a farm but also "an entrepreneurial nonprofit organization that inspires people and communities to embrace integrated solutions for sustainable development."

Alas, it turns out that in today's economic times, being sustainable isn't so sustainable. The farm was put up for sale in 2008 after the Le Vans tired of the time and exorbitant expense of building, health and safety process required today. Yet, work on a ranch never stops.

When I visited Sustainable Settings, I crossed Thompson Creek drainage and entered a compound full of energy and activity. Ever busy, Brook took time to

The Ute Connection: Alex Thompson, here with wife, Jane, was one of the first settlers to live among the Crystal River Valley Utes. Thompsons worked their land from 1893 to 1949. The Thompson Ranch achieved a modicum of modernity when the new lowline ditch and steam powered thrasher came along in 1919. Courtesy of Sustainable Settings

share with me some of the stories he's been told by four generations to come back to the Thompson homestead.

RAW, RICH LAND AND FRIENDLY NATIVES

Dad Myron and son Alex Thompson came out from Michigan City, Indiana around 1876 when land in the Rockies was "raw," Brook said. Raw and very rich, because of beavers, some thousands of years ago, that dammed and flooded the valley, turning it into fertile, naturally organic mountain soil.

Many a family story told under the roof of the Thompson "Big House" was of how, as early as 1876, Myron and Alex not only got along but ran around with

Since 2003, Sustainable Settings has resurrected local production of meat, poultry, dairy and vegetables at the Thompson Creek Ranch by intertwining old and new approaches to agriculture. Courtesy of Sustainable Settings

the Utes. Father and son were aware and understood the potential of the land but at the time worked as miners.

"The Utes were friendly, traded with them, shared their hunting grounds, food, water and edible plants." Brook remembered being told by a Thompson. "There was a bridge of time when the Utes and whites got along." That important knowledge was why after the Utes were driven out of their homeland and the government implemented the Homestead Act in 1882, the Thompson men knew right where to go, to use the land in the wisest way possible.

LIFE IN THE (LITTLE) BIG HOUSE

The side-by-side Thompson and Thompson ranches eventually produced some twenty-two train car loads of potatoes from their land when the railroad used to stop at the neighboring Sewell Ranch depot. Brook said that when Alex sold a right-of-way across the Thompson land to the railroad for the sum of two thousand dollars—a serious amount of money back in 1892—that money went to build a "modern" home, the so-named "Big House." The home's original square footage is unknown, though the Le Vans now live in the enlarged twelve hundred square foot version. Indications are that the Thompsons used their trusty Sears and Roebuck catalog to order building materials from back East and accessorized their home with ornate trim work still intact today.

Brook told of how Eva Cochrane, a Thompson granddaughter, came by for a visit awhile back. "Eva took me out to the homestead cabin fronting [Highway] 133, wagged her finger at me and said, 'Now I'm not going to tell you how old I am, but I was born upstairs in the attic of that cabin and lived there until I was twenty-one years old.'"

Fresh baked bread with butter and sugar was a rare and favorite treat of Eva's when she was a little girl. She also remembered the coal room under the kitchen where carbide stones were kept for the first carbide-lighted ranch house "so remote" from Carbondale. Eva also remarked how it took an hour by horse to get that long five miles into town.

Let's muse on that thought. Five miles in one hour. One-horse powered. Today, we think nothing of strapping ourselves onto more like three hundred and fifty horses and away we go!

ANGELINA'S SWEETEST MILK

Brook told me that the Mautz family bought the ranch from the Thompsons in 1949 and carried on the farming and dairy production that Angelina Mautz became famous for until 1992 when the ranch was sold. Folks all around appreciated the sweet, fresh milk from Angelina's cows.

The land lay fallow under a developer's plan for eleven mega-houses from 1992 until Pitkin County Open Space intervened. Rose, Brook and Sustainable Settings came along and brought it back to life in 2003. They wanted to add a dairy but regulations required made that untenable. Too bad.

MORE YAKKING

"Brook, what's the story about those cute yaks we see out there in the field when we drive by?"

"Crystal Valley's cattle raising has only been around for the past hundred and fifty years or so," said Brook. "Cattle are not indigenous to high altitudes," he continued. "They were brought here along with sheep and goats by the Spaniards and other Europeans when they came over the Rockies."

BUT DO THEY MOO?

On the other hand, "…yaks are naturally high-altitude bovines with a high red blood cell count. Their meat is between elk and beef in flavor," Brook explained, "lean like elk and not cross-bred." He added, "…and yaks are fence-friendly."

"No kidding!" yelped this pseudo-daring writer. I nearly got a long-tongued wet smooch by a young yak as I snapped these fence line shots. This yak family was the closest to the highway I'd seen for awhile so I made a U-turn that morning and came back, which was well worth the extra five minutes it took.

Up close and personal visit with the friendly yaks of Sustainable Settings Ranch. Author photo

Hummm. Note to self: Slow down, seize the moment and appreciate this special place whenever you can.

"…and what we've learned is they eat one-third less, making them a lighter feed burden," continued Brook. "They are smaller, but this is a niche market item. We expect to slaughter and process the first..."

"Wha-a-a-t? Wait a minute! Market item?"

The light in the refrigerator went on. Oh my. Of course.

"Yes, we produce 'food,'" Brook said, chuckling as my naïve realization went from cute to, uh, choice cuts. He didn't miss a beat though. "We will soon have the first 'beyond organic' yak burger available for sale."

Sustainable Settings does a brisk business with farm-raised poultry, eggs and turkeys. Most turkeys are sold out by August for Thanksgiving each year. By June, all but a few birds are strutting about the grounds with a tag. (And here the few unadorned are wondering, 'why don't I have a sparkly "necklace" like Myrtle's?')

AVAILABILITY REQUIRED FOR SUSTAINABILITY

The first two-leggeds that lived here knew that by the old ways, reliance on sustenance from this land began with education and appreciation of the gifts given by Mother Nature. There is a memorable Native American saying about planning out seven generations for their children. The number of years between grandchild becoming grandparent comes better into perspective when Brook reminded me that at least four generations of the Thompson clan have returned to visit the this old homestead of 1881.

Imagine this: Once upon a time, this ranchland used to produce all the food needed by the families living here. Given the difficulties that Sustainable Settings has encountered with the expense and scope of today's governmental regulations, we have to wonder, not only what will the land look like but how will these once-food-producing acres of the Crystal River Valley be remembered by our children's grandchildren?

Chapter 7

SWISS VILLAGE RESORT

Readers will remember how BRB Resort and Campground started in the early sixties by the Texas-bred Burketts. Remember BRB? It's the last place up the mountain road where cell phones work ...or what some call "the beginning of peace and quiet."

WHAT DID THE TEXANS KNOW?

After years of fishing, hunting and camping in this valley, the Dallas-area folks decided to build BRB Resort just outside of Carbondale in the 60s. But the Burketts were trumped by yet another Texas-transplanted family of fishermen and hunters. Wallace Parker's folks built the Swiss Village Resort in Redstone in 1949.

Wallace and his wife, Naomi graciously visited with me one evening in their home. Wallace was still in his coveralls, having come home from a full-day's work building a house in Aspen.

Let the math part of your brain kick in here. This writer had only opened her eyes to some three hundred mornings in life when Wallace was pounding nails and building cabins with his parents in 1949. And here he is today, still building houses, cleaning up mudslides, whatever needs done. Hard physical work is no stranger to Wallace. Many younger could only aspire.

One of Swiss Village cabins next to Gamekeepers Lodge, Spring of '49.

Family pet, Tuffy, inspects the sign for the brand new Swiss Village Resort, Redstone, Colorado, circa 1950. Photos courtesy of Parker collection

"Guess you are here to learn how Swiss Village came to be," Wallace said, settling back into a comfortable brown leather recliner, with a hint of a smile and a memory or two behind those charming blue eyes.

THE LAND OF LEDERHOSEN AND STREUDL? NOT!

"The story began in the late nineteen thirties," Wallace began. "Father accompanied a man from Fort Worth to San Luis Valley to pick up a load of potatoes. It sparked an interest in Colorado." Wallace's gentle voice lowered into a cadence that transcended present time.

"Their paint-manufacturing business kept Father and Mother in Fort Worth, but it was our dream to have a summer resort one day up in the mountains. Rustic cabins with an outhouse, water pumped into a bucket outside, woodburning stoves...that was about it back then. We dreamt of a place with running water inside, a bathroom, propane cookstove and Servel Electrolux refrigerators."

Wallace's father wrote letters to the chambers of commerce of the family's areas of interest, primarily around the southwest part of Colorado. "One of the Realtors we met was a gentleman by the name of Jarvis in Durango. He mentioned his son was getting ready to sell the Gamekeeper's Lodge in Redstone and how he too, always dreamed of someday making it into a resort that they would call 'Swiss Village.'"

"WOULD YOU LIKE TO TAKE A LOOK?"

Wallace and his parents made that serendipitous trip upvalley the first week of June 1948. They fell in love with the home built as a replica of an Austrian ski lodge, not to mention the ten acres on which it sat next to the old John Cleveland Osgood barn. They stood a stone's throw across the Crystal River from what was called back then, "The Mansion." "It wasn't called the [Redstone] 'Castle' until more recently," Wallace said.

They were told how Osgood kept deer, elk and bighorn sheep on the property and in the early days, fed them from the hay stored in the barn.

Let's sidestep a moment here for readers not yet familiar with the history of Redstone. The Osgood name was what put Redstone on the map at the turn of the twentieth century. Osgood's wealth and regard for his employees and coalmining interests, created the village, its services and homes for his workers and their families. However, by the time the Parkers arrived forty-some years later, Redstone was out of work, mostly empty and very quiet.

"There were fewer than fifteen year-round families from the twenty miles between Sewells [outside of Carbondale] up to Marble at that time," said Wallace. "We had hand-crank telephones. All of us were on the only party line. I can still name most of them, even now," he mused. "As the years passed it got down to an eight-party line, and eventually in the mid to late sixties, we got a private line for the resort."

Meanwhile, that June day was the beginning and the end of Parkers' search. They didn't look at anything else. They made up their minds and purchased the Gamekeeper's Lodge before they returned to Texas.

Their dream manifested the following March of 1949, when the Parkers loaded up a trailer full of supplies and headed for Redstone. They quickly built three small cabins and remodeled the barn into three units.

On Fourth of July weekend 1949, the Parkers officially opened Swiss Village Resort. Their first guests were the Silversteins from Denver who forked over eight bucks for a night in a two-bedded cabin.

"Or they could have the cabin for fifty dollars a week," said Wallace, grinning. "Even by the time we sold the lodge to Jeff Bier in 1976, when we were up to sixty-five dollars a week, it couldn't buy you a half a night's sleep today."

THE BOOMING FIFTIES

Wallace told how in the early fifties, it was easy to ascertain the progress of Holy Cross Energy, which was digging the electric line to bring service up to Marble. Seems that whenever they would hit rock—in these *rocky* mountains—they'd set off dynamite charges. With nary a regulation or permit required, or even imagined back then, rocks could suddenly fall out of the sky at anytime, anywhere. Guests out for a day's adventure by horse or Jeep learned to duck first, then look around.

DAY TRIPS: WATCH YOUR HEAD

Wallace said he remembers watching a geyser blow after a set charge exploded nearby. Oops. The "rock" this charge was set against was actually a four-inch cast iron water main for "the mansion." Holy Cross had to dig a hole to repair the break in the line, which they did with oakum and lead wool.

The Parkers offered day trips to their guests...Jeep tours of Coal Basin, and up through Marble to the Yule Quarry, and Crystal City.

Wallace shared how they could do anything they wanted and go anywhere they wanted in those days. So there were requests for lots of trips through the Coal Basin townsite where many of the cone-pitched homes were still intact. Wallace remembered how there was still writing on a few of the old school's chalkboards. Same with the households; everything sitting out on tables and such. He said that it was as though the Coal Basin residents went for a walk and never came back.

When they traveled to Crystal, they would always stop at one of two soda pop stands in Marble, which was about all the activity there was in Marble after the quarry closed in 1941. One stand belonged to Teresa Hermann, the local schoolteacher, but the stand was named Ken's Pop Stand, after her son. Rome and Ruby Isler had the other stand. Always thinking of others during the seasonal tourist time, Wallace would take turns giving business to each.

"Year-round, though, the only residents in Marble back then were Teresa, the Orloskys and John Darien," Wallace said. Darien's claim to fame was his care of the county roads up to Crystal, which made the roads back to Crystal at least passable by vehicle. Darien lived and died upstairs in the Marble City State Bank building during the time when it had been converted into a county mechanic's garage.

The Gameskeepers Lodge today sits across Highway 133 and the Crystal River from Osgood's mansion, later called the Redstone Castle.

Wallace also remembered the time that he was walking through the remains of the Marble Millsite Park and National Historical Site today. He picked up from the ground, part of the schematic plans for the Lincoln Memorial...and put them back down. Could have you or I?

Another interest-

View of Coalbasin c. 1904. "By 1902, 265 men were employed at Coalbasin, mostly Austrians, Italians and Slavs as well as native-born Americans," according to Dell McCoy, "*Crystal River Pictorial*," Sundance Publications Ltd.

ing trip Wallace remembered was up to the marble quarry which, at that time, had been closed but a few years earlier. The workers' residences, called Quarrytown, clung to the side of the hill near the Yule mine entrance. "They were box houses," he said. The bunkhouse was still mostly upright, with wood by the stove and clothes hanging on the wall, as though the wearer would soon be back after work. Sheets of newspapers of the day were pasted on the walls, the only insulation against the board and batt walls holding up the roof. It had to be unbelievably cold no matter what they did.

Wallace said all the guests looked forward to the trips to the quarry. The more adventurous would climb down the quarry walls to explore the dark interiors. "They also enjoyed picnics at Lead King Basin, Crystal and Geneva Lake," he added.

Swiss Village Resort's business grew rapidly because sports and city editors for Dallas and Fort Worth newspapers raved to its avid fishermen and hunters the bounty to be found in the Crystal River Valley. For whatever reason, the Texas, Oklahoma and California visitors primarily bunched up in August and Wallace remembered how it took awhile for the bookings to spread out.

"August was the only month until they discovered July," he said. Of course, September was always a good month because of hunting season and Wallace's father was a popular licensed guide. As the years passed, Wallace and his folks built more and more cabins until they had a dozen cabins all together. In 1952, Naomi and Wallace married and she became an enlisted helper too.

MOVING ON DOWN THE ROAD...

In 1959 another change came to the Redstone community. Wallace said Frank Kistler, who owned the Glenwood Springs Lodge, bought the Redstone Inn, the Mansion, Redstone Ranch Acres, the Haskell Ranch and quite a few other properties around Redstone. Kistler did not want the resort in the middle of his newly-purchased property so the story goes that he offered a nice price for the Gamekeeper's Lodge, with the condition that the guest cabins would be taken off the site.

That fall, the Parkers started looking for another location for Swiss Village Resort. They came across Avalanche Ranch, a half a dozen miles below Redstone.

Situated on the west side of the river, Avalanche Ranch was closer to Carbondale. Folks whizzing through the curves of 133 today don't realize what the road was like fifty years ago. (Hey, that's not that long ago anymore!)

"This road was very rough, just dirt and some gravel," Wallace said. "Especially after a dry spell, you could still see the crossties for the old railroad bed where the rails had been pulled up in the late forties. We got to learn where the bad spots were so we could drive around them and keep from hitting the spikes with our tires."

Perhaps the closest first-hand experience today would be for those folks who have traversed the Marble road up Daniels Hill and over to Crystal City. They might have a more vivid picture of Wallace's description of Highway 133.

BUT WAS IT MISSION IMPOSSIBLE?

By spring thaw, Wallace said they managed to have the resort operational in its new location for the summer of 1960's vacationers. Avalanche Ranch had reincarnated into Swiss Village Resort during the winter. Makes this writer wonder what stories there must be of how they transported six to eight cabins over the rough dirt road of Highway 133, with winter and spring weather conditions prevailing.

One summer, the returning families were pleasantly surprised to find a bathhouse and central water. A few years later, the Parkers added a recreation room. Swiss Village Resort continued in its new home for another fifteen or sixteen years until the place was sold in 1976 and the name reverted back to Avalanche Ranch. Today, the resort is operated by the Ogilby family, who also own the place next door, Hell Roaring Ranch.

Meanwhile, before that first mountain snow that comes every October, the Parkers headed back to Fort Worth, alongside southbound hummingbirds, counting months off the calendar until they returned again to this special place.

It reminds this writer to acknowledge and honor all the ancestors and all those before us, who appreciate the beauty here. Wallace described it thus:

"Many places have a beautiful spot to go to and look at...not like this, where mile after mile, there is even more beautiful scenery that unfolds. The higher you go, the more you are impressed by this valley."

A LITTLE HARD WORK AND LOTS OF FUN

In 1961, after Wallace had taught school in Texas for ten years, he and Naomi decided to move to the Crystal Valley full-time. They had four daughters to raise by then. He became principal of the Roaring Fork High School in Carbondale.

"Come summer though, we all worked in the business," Naomi said. "The girls cleaned cabins and helped out around the place. It was always a family affair."

In fact, relatives coming to spend the summer were sure to be pressed into service; cooking, guiding, getting to know and entertaining the guests, who usually stayed anywhere from a week to a month. After all, folks didn't have much money back then, Wallace reminds us. They would save up all year for their main expense—gas. They'd bring the food they would eat at home anyway, and enjoy the respite of a cool, colorful Colorado.

Preston Parker, Wallace's cousin, wrote to me, "I remember when my father [Wallace's brother] built our own cabin...it was moved, along with the others, to the new location. When Dad retired in 1959, he and Mom spent every summer [at Swiss Village] until the sale in '76.

"I, too, was a teacher and an administrator, so my family spent many vacations in the Crystal Valley," Preston said. "The Crystal River is still my favorite 'fishing hole' in all the world."

A very reasonable vacation destination, it wasn't long before several groups of friends and families spent their summers at Swiss Village Resort. In fact, Wallace said that Lane Stewart, whose wonderful western portraits hang in the Redstone Inn Bar and Grill today, is the son of a family who came for twenty-five of the twenty-six years the Swiss Village Resort was in operation.

"Most everyone made their reservations for the next year as they came to say goodbye." Naomi said. "They attended all our daughters' weddings and the girls would go down to Texas to visit. We became like family to each other."

Wallace agreed. After showing me a few early-day photos, he sat back in his recliner. "It was a very pleasant business," he said. "We never had to ask anyone to leave, we never had to ask anyone to not come back." His eyes locked into mine. Uh, you mean...until tonight? The grandfather clock tolled nine times. Yikes. Where had time gone? The Parkers were saints of patience as I encouraged their memories of days gone by up the Crystal.

Wallace had told me earlier on that their day starts early. As I passed through Naomi's kitchen and out the door, I saw the biggest collection of chicken memorabilia I had ever seen. No wonder they are used to getting up with the chickens, so's to speak.

Chapter 8

MARBLE MEMORIAL AIRPORT

The aerial photo of our landing is again courtesy of "Mr. Eagle" Rob Hunker and ColoradoAerialViews.com. We're coming in, facing west, and downstream of the upper Crystal River Valley. County Road 3 is to the right, the river to the left of our view. Ladies and gentlemen, fasten your seatbelts.

WELCOME TO MARBLE MEMORIAL AIRPORT!

ALRIGHT! We've landed, upright and safely at the last privately-owned, open to the public, high-altitude grass airstrip in Colorado. Please stay in your seats, folks, until we come to a full stop.

We taxi up the grassy airstrip to a shaded table under Ponderosa pine trees and RV-vacation home of Robert and Patty Conger of Denver. The picnic table affords a cool, comfortable observation station to the comings and goings of folks up and down the valley, whether by Jeep, bike or bi-plane.

As Bob, Patty and I sit down together, a flock of winged relations in our valley, Canadian geese, swoop in and gather at one area by the pond. They begin pecking and pooping en masse.

"Bob, this looks like a natural spot for an airstrip," I said. "How did it first come to be?"

"That goes back to Wade Loudermilk, who was a pilot," said Bob. "He also had excavating equipment so he put in the airstrip in '55-'56. Loudermilk flew a Cessna 180 and owned a little cabin across the Hermits Hideaway bridge. He would land, taxi across the bridge and tie down the plane in his front yard."

Soon another pilot, John Freeman, flew into Marble in his Piper Aztec to access his remote cabin just off the road to Lead King Basin, followed by Harry Lodge, a prep school dean at Forest Lake Academy in Maitland, Florida. Lodge's family settled in the then-ghost town of Crystal City and today they still own land and properties in the area, including the famous Crystal Mill.

JUST ANOTHER COINCIDENCE YOU SAY?

Veteran pilot Bob Conger came along in 1982 in his Maule M-5 bush plane. Turns out, he, John and Harry were Seventh-Day Adventists (SDA), having spent overlapping years at the same prep school, which happened to be Forest Lake Academy. They lived within seven miles of each other in Marble and didn't know it. That is until one day, a connection was made by Sue Blue, wife of airstrip caretaker Kirk (their story in Chapter 13, the Heartbreak Hotel story.) Sue told Bob, "You have to meet these fellows. You all tell the same stories about school!"

The men reunited and enjoyed many SDA church services and potlucks in Crystal City. They were soon joined by fellow Adventists Bonnie and Leland Stanford, III, who had a Crystal cabin. Bob said they were related to the Stanfords who built a little university in California.

So, here are three men who knew each other during their Florida high school days then lose contact. Thinking of one or two of your classmates? Later on two of them became pilots and some twenty or thirty years later, between the late fifties and early eighties, all three chose this particular remote valley in Colorado to make their vacation homes. Just another of many Crystal Valley coincidences.

Today the airstrip is a popular destination for mountain pilots. The Colorado Pilots Association hosts an annual fly-in. The pilots enjoy visiting and talking about their planes, so be sure to stop if you are in the area during their rendezvous.

RIGHT PLACE, RIGHT TIME

Bob Conger loved what he saw in the early-eighties era of Marble. He purchased the airstrip and some surrounding acreage from past-due notes and back taxes in the late seventies tied to a resort known as the Marble Ski Area. The ski area, and its ambitious plan to become the link between prestigious Aspen and Crested Butte ski resorts, was one of the most controversial developments in the history of this dead-end canyon, its own chapter one day.

Bob said he has been coming up to Marble every chance he can get since—a good respite for the Denver businessman.

He showed burn scars on both of his hands, memorable evidence of the dark side in the joy of flying when his plane caught fire. Bob no longer flies.

Aerial view of Marble Memorial Airport, facing west (top). County Road 3 curves to the right of the strip. Crystal River on left, McGhee Pond on the right center. At top end of strip is the bridge to Hermits Hideaway (left) and Crystal Meadows (top) subdivisions. Further west is Ute Meadows, now in a conservation easement by Great Outdoors Colorado (GOCO). Courtesy of Rob Hunker, www.ColoradoAerialViews.com

"Accidents happen," Bob said. He turned his hands, and memories, over and back. "That is why this is named the Marble Memorial Airport, for my daughter, Lillian and her family. Their plane crashed in Salmon, Idaho." He paused, "I didn't fly after that and sold my plane after awhile."

As he looked across the pond at a distant point, Patty put her hand over his. They gazed at each other, full of mature understanding, albeit with the energy of young lovers.

"SNOW" HEART IN MARBLE

"How long have you two been married?" I asked.

They both smiled broadly and Bob answered without hesitation, "We've been together seventeen years and celebrated our sixth anniversary the end of June." He hugged his bride even closer on the picnic bench. Patty beamed back. "And Bob's birthday was yesterday," she said.

Looks like I'd arrived in the middle of multiple celebrations at the Conger compound. Three camper trailers were lined up beneath Ponderosa pines alongside the grassy airstrip. The other two were for family and guests. Patty and Bob

53

The airstrip facing east towards Sheep (left) and Whitehouse (right) Mountains. The Crystal River is on the right beyond the willows. The Conger compound in the pine trees on the right. Author photo

have a fifth-wheel trailer closest to their pond. A two-seated wood swing set, a gift from the kids, looks over the pond with a wide-angle panorama into the eastern Crystal Valley. Wow, what a view!

"This is where we got married," Bob continued. "See up there on Whitehouse Mountain?" Bob pointed directly ahead to the bare mountain top. "It has only happened a couple of times where a patch of snow, as it melts, looks exactly like a heart, with a hole in it..."

"...where the arrow went," Patty chimed in. "and it happened that June we married."

"Our friends were almost convinced I had something to do with intentionally putting the snow there," Bob said chuckling. Maybe Bob has been known to move mountains when he sets his mind to it? Bob shared that, even though he and Patty are good friends with his ex'es, he struck out in the matrimonial batter box a couple times. He believes the third time's a charm.

BETTER LATE THAN NEVER!

"So then, how did you meet?" I persisted. This sounded like a fun story!

Patty spoke next. "We lived in apartments in a brownstone in Loveland back in 1954 with our respective spouses for a period of time," she said. "In 1965, my husbad and I moved to Aspen and lost contact with the Conger family."

One day twenty-some years later, Bob's sister, Sarah Cushing, gave him a clipping of an obituary. "We tend to read those more often as we get older," Bob mused. Patty's husband had passed away. Bob kept the folded newspaper clipping in his wallet, thinking that some time he'd like to look Patty up and express his condolences.

Awhile, "maybe a year" later, he was in Carbondale for a meeting for the Marble Metro District. He remembered reading in the clipping that Patty's daughter, Karen and son-in-law, John Salamida lived in Carbondale and owned (and still do) a silkscreen tee shirt design store called The Shirt Stop.

"I called and asked John to pass on to Karen's mother that I'd like to get in touch for old time's sake."

Days. Weeks. Months. Not a word from Patty.

ANOTHER COINCIDENCE? HOW MANY DOES HE GET?

As the story goes, little did Bob know at the time, but someone dropped the ball. Daughter and son-in-law completely forgot about passing on the message.

Bob let it go. But somehow, if not in person, Patty kept coming up in his thoughts. At the time, she owned the Yampah Vapor Caves in Glenwood Springs. Bob said that on one of his business trips from Denver to Salt Lake City, he was passing through Glenwood around noontime. He impulsively decided to drop in at the caves to see if Patty would like to go to lunch.

"If she didn't want to see me then, well, that was fine," said Bob. It took a good bit of convincing a protective front desk person to ask Patty to come down from her upstairs apartment without identifying who was calling on her.

"I wanted to surprise her."

Turns out Patty had sold the vapor caves and was packing that day—one of her last there.

Colorado Pilots Association annual fly-in at the Marble Memorial Airport, usually the first week of September. The pilots love to talk about their planes and welcome visitors during their stay. Coutesy of Conger collection

55

"She came downstairs with those twinkly brown eyes," Bob said. He knew all was right with the world.

Patty remembered her first thought on seeing Bob in the lobby.

"I happened to read a newspaper astrology column on my November 1989 birthday. It said, 'You will meet someone in March 1990 who will be around for a long time.' "

Their first date? March 1990. One could easily see by this happy, loving couple that Bob made a good right turn when he pulled into the vapor caves parking lot that particular day.

LOVE ON THE MENU WITH CHINESE AND A WHISKEY SOUR

Patty went on. "It was good to see him. He asked me out to lunch and we had Chinese," she said. "He asked if I'd like something to drink. I felt very sophisticated when I told the waiter, 'Whiskey sour, please.' It was the only mixed drink I had ever had, going back in my twenties."

Bob, who just so happened to own a bar, knew "no one drank whiskey sours anymore." He fell even more in love.

Theirs was a long-distance romance for a year and a half with, of course, two different versions. Bob said, "I like mine best. One day Patty came to see me and never left."

Eleven years after their first date, they officially tied the knot in front of Whitehouse Mountain's "snow heart." And their hearts are obviously tied to Marble.

Patty nudged Bob. "What's that you say whenever we turn up County Road 3?"

"This is the place where my bones feel the most comfortable," replied Bob. He hugged his bride again. "This may not be heaven but you can see it from here."

Chapter 9

MARBLE SHEEP RUN

RING! R-i-i-n-g! R-i-i-i-n-n-g-g-g! Rippling through the river fog of an early morn, telephones around Marble were ringing off their hooks.

"Wha…? Who's calling? Why so early?" grumbled a number of folks this cool autumn dawn. On the other end of the line was the slow, southern drawl of one Charlie Manus of Marble.

"Uh, hi. The sheep are running this morning."

Don't know about the other households that were called, but this writer's beloved… ahem…answered. "Yeah, okay," hung up and went back to sleep.

All returned to stillness…but for the sound of one very rapid heartbeat. That would be mine.

SUSPENDED MOMENT IN TIME—WHAT TO DO?

"Excuse me!" Always a good way to awaken your partner. "What was that all about?"

"Thesheeparecomin'," came the pillowed mumble.

"Now? NOW? C'mon! We've got to go!" I yelled.

With hair-on-fire speed, we made it up Connie Hendrix' and Charlie Manus' driveway in time to join other barely-awakes for front row seats at the Mimosas-on-the-Deck sheep-watching event.

"Here they come!" Connie shouted. Someone handed us a Mimosa.

SHEEP POO AND CHAMPAGNE—ONLY IN MARBLE

A horseman led the procession, flanked by two flashing black and white units; that is, Border collies. They dutifully paced back and forth across the road, keeping the frisky sheep on track.

The first band of three—meaning some three thousand-plus ewes and lambs—barreled, baa-aa-ed, and cavorted over each other down the dirt road. On the sidelines, a gaggle of two-leggeds pointed flashing boxes.

"Whew, that was really short notice, Connie!" I said. "One more minute, and we would have been stuck on the other side of the parade [i.e. the non-refreshment side]. How did you find out today was THE day?" I sniffed the air, zeroing in on the general direction of the caffeine pot. "By the way, where's that coffee?"

NO TIME FOR RSVPS

"That's been part of the fun every year!" said Connie. "When will we know? How do we find out?

"Usually the sheep cross over County Road 3 onto the airstrip," she continued. "With the pilots' fly-in this weekend, we all thought it would happen next week. But there was a phone message on our machine last night that said it would be today," Connie said, giggling. "We knew we shouldn't try to call folks that late so Charlie started at 6:30 this morning."

Connie has an adorable giggle. It is infectious. No wonder Charlie could bite the bullet and call friends and neighbors at that unseemly hour, at least for a weekend morning. "Charlie kept dialing numbers as we thought of them."

A couple times, Connie said, Charlie hung up with a shrug of his shoulders. "This one sounded disgruntled. Think I woke 'em up," he'd call out.

"But, you know," Connie said, "all came. All are jovial and that shows they're good sports...and all look good." She beamed as she looked around the crowded deck.

Coveted coffee cup in one hand, I bit into a warm slice of frittata, one of many breakfast offerings on the picnic table such as smoked salmon, nut bread and fresh fruit. "You mean to say you put on this whole spread in an hour?" I asked.

"I had planned to go shopping downvalley next Monday," said Connie. "So, it was into the refrigerator and freezer for whatever I could find this morning. A dozen eggs. Enough for this frittata. Two cans of frozen orange juice...."

One of the first neighbors Charlie called had offered up a couple bottles of champagne, so in short order, Connie and Charlie had an instant "Mimosas-on-the-Deck" sheep-watching party. Move over, Martha Stewart. Talk about knowing how to stock a backcountry pantry and invite friends bearing goodies. Oh yes, indeed, ready for any excuse for a jolly good time up in the mountains.

"Maybe it's the time of day or something that makes it different than our usual get togethers. It's a lot of fun, " Connie said. "I recall one particular year, another Tuesday morning. We were all happy and jovial on the deck then too."

That year, 2001, after the sheep passed, a neighbor came over to report, "We're at war." It was 9/11.

Get Ready...Get Set...Go! Photo by Connie Hendrix.

"We realized as we all gathered around the television that it was comforting to be together," said Connie.

WRITING HISTORY MEMOIRS ISN'T JUST ABOUT THE PARTIES

High-octane caffeine coursed through my bloodstream, jolting my brain into action. "Whose sheep are they? Where are they going? How long have they been doing this?"

Connie propelled me onward in my search for sheep stories. "We got a call from someone who knew someone else who said to call someone else for Joe Sperry's phone number," she said. "They're his sheep coming through."

O—kay! With no zippy text-messaging up here, I caught up with Mr. Sperry on the old can-and-string method. "Hi, Joe. So, how long have you been a, uh, ah, ...?"

"A sheep man," Joe replied, helping me out (whew). "I'm a newcomer, just since 1970. You'd need to talk to the Bairs for history." The Bair family, particularly Elmer Bair, is a name synonymous with sheepherding in this valley.

Joe continued.

"My folks were in cattle and I grew up that way," he said. "Then we expanded into sheep. I eventually got my first band of sheep, about six hundred ewes and

Sheepherders near the end of the dusty trail and a summer caring for their flocks above Marble. Photo by Connie Hendrix

maybe twelve hundred lambs." Joe ended up with some of Elmer Bair's old permits when the U.S. Forest Service became comfortable with his operation methods. Operations that include summer grazing in the Snowmass Maroon Bells Wilderness above Marble.

"We move from Daly, Lost Trail Creek, across Lead King Basin and Fravert Basin, over Schofield Basin, Belleview Mountain and Mount Belleview." Joe said.

He confirmed that current bands total some three thousand ewes and lambs. They can be spread out anywhere from a hundred and fifty to two hundred acres over a day's time. But at night when they are all bedded down, it's wool-to-wool blanketing maybe one to ten acres. Acres? Do our readers often get to see an acre of sleeping sheep, let alone ten or two hundred at one time?

"Do you move all these sheep, Joe?" I asked.

"No, Flavio is the man," Joe said. "He has been with me since 1980, when he was nineteen years old." Flavio's brother, Agripin, has also herded for Joe since back in the seventies and helped again this year.

"Flavio is up there for about sixty days each summer," Joe said. "After we finish separating out the herd in Collbran, he heads for Mexico in the winter. Come spring, he's back to help us down in Delta with the lambing, which is his specialty."

IT'S A DOG'S LIFE

I asked Joe about the dogs that accompany the bands. There is no question about the importance of Border collies with respect to their jobs. Those black and white patrollers miss not one errant lamb. Their focus and herding techniques are always a delight to watch. This year, we noticed a large, lanky white blond dog in the group. He appeared to be taking a nonchalant morning stroll alongside the spirited parade.

"They are called Akbash. They live with the sheep," Joe explained. "They don't herd, they guard."

And they protect against...? "There are mountain lions, bears, coyotes, bobcats; even a pair of foxes have been spotted taking down a thirty-pound lamb." Joe said.

Akbash, the Turkish name for "white head," are bred to live among and guard the sheep while on the range. Photo by Connie Hendrix

We have all heard about the increased bear activity from Aspen to Redstone and Marble. Joe gave us some current bear statistics that are sobering.

He compared two recent years of attrition where sheep die for various reasons: weather, illness, predators, poison, etc. In the first year, there were fifty-six lambs and thirty-eight ewes killed. In the second year, there were two hundred and two lambs and sixty-three ewes killed. In the first, bear attacks were sporadic but in the second year, there were two solid months of bear predation.

Folks mostly don't realize the significance of predator problems to the sheep man. A 5 to 15 percent reduction of the band can represent something like twenty thousand dollars in losses. That's a lot of lamb chops not going to market.

Then there are the losses that defy explanation. Joe told of an incident that happened to his herder one year. The herder had gone out a distance to check for strays when he saw two backpackers coming out of the trees with their dogs off-leash.

Before the herder could get back, the dogs had chased some of the band into a narrow draw, where the spooked sheep piled on top of each other. While the herder was able to save forty or fifty, more than twenty sheep were killed by suffocation.

"People don't realize that sometimes they can't control their dogs like they think," said Joe.

The backpackers put their pets on leashes and quietly disappeared over the hill. Joe knows that the Forest Service rules of dogs on leash are for good reasons. "The Forest Service does a very good job of administering these lands," he said, "even spread as thin as they are.

BUT THIS IS THE SAME SPOT...TWICE!

I asked Joe about other incidents that come to mind. You know that old saying, lightning never strikes the same place twice? Well, don't say that in front of Flavio. He'll beg to differ. Seems there is one certain ridge where lightning strikes happen a little too often for his comfort. On two different occasions, a ewe and two lambs were struck and Flavio was knocked clear out of his bed. There were five holes in the tent where the flashes hit. Some of the canned goods were arced together from the force. Needless to say, summer storms don't bode well with this shepherd.

"All in all, being a sheep man is a way of life that is part of the tradition of the

A four-wheeler replaces four-legged horsepower needed to quickly herd sheep between pedestrian and vehicular traffic that grows exponentially every year between the sheep and their destination. Photo by Connie Hendrix

country," Joe said. It is a way of working with the eco-system where renewable resources—the sheep—use the land, alternately public and private, without ruining it by over- or under-grazing, because of more prudent management. The win-win-win relationship between wildlife, ranchers, and coordination with the Forest Service working hand-in-hand gives Joe the satisfaction of knowing he carries on a legacy of careful, thoughtful husbandry of these natural resources. Even if his thirty-some years in the biz still makes him a short-timer.

TALK TO A BAIR ABOUT SHEEP? YEAH, SURE

We go in search of Elmer Bair's family for more sheep background. Turns out Dominique Needham, daughter of Elmer's granddaughter Jeri, owns a hair salon in Carbondale—Salon Sublime—where I just so happen to get my locks refreshed. In the wash basin area, there's a big black and white photo of Ida, Elmer's wife and Dominique's great grandma; head full of perm curlers in a hair salon circa the nineteen forties. I'm in the right place!

"Granddad wrote a book, I'll get it for you, all about our family's life here," she said.

Elmer Bair's Story, 1899-1987 is nearly five hundred pages of the most interesting, compelling, hilarious stories "...written in the language of [an] ol' sheepherder," according to Elmer.

Elmer came to Marble in 1926 because Ida's family, including parents, brothers and sisters and their families, were living in Marble.

"There were plenty of opportunities working with sheep, but it would have taken me away from my family. I was offered a job with the Yule Marble Company, working in the quarry, and I accepted it," Elmer wrote. "We rented a house in Marble and started making preparations for the winter." He eventually helped load and carry down the "Big Rock" of marble that was cut into the Tomb of the Unknown Soldier and placed in Arlington Cemetery.

But Elmer's heart was set on acquiring a sheep outfit of his own, he wrote, and in the summer of 1931 it looked as though that time had come. His down-to-earth details keep the reader spellbound. Showdowns with armed cattlemen. Wildfires, coyotes and really hungry bears, oh my.

After they settled in Carbondale, the Bairs built a summer home up on their old sheep range in Marble and the cabin was a safe haven from all the cares and concerns of the world. He meant it to stay in the family. "We hope our descendents will always treat it as a hallowed spot and enjoy it with their descendents." He referred to a poem by H. R. Merrill to describe their home's site.

OH, GOD, LET THIS BE HEAVEN

Oh God, let this be heaven.
I do not ask for golden streets,
Or long for jasper walls,
Nor do I sigh for pearly shores,
Where twilight never falls;
Just leave me here besides these ol' peaks'
In this rough western land —
I love this dear old world of thine
Dear God, you understand.

Oh, God, let this be heaven.
I do not ask for angel wings,
Just leave that old peak there,
And let me climb 'till comes the night.
I want no golden stairs, then when I say my last adieu,
And all farewells are given,
Just leave my spirit here somewhere—
Dear God, let this be heaven.

Chapter 10

MARBLE'S "GODPOTTER"—
THANOS JOHNSON

Remember Anthony Quinn in *Zorba the Greek*? Well, Zorba times ten described Thanos Johnson. Like Zorba, Thanos was the classic, curly-headed, bearded Greek, a lover of fine food, wine and art with an intense pride of his Hellenic heritage.

OPA! OPA! CELEBRATE LIFE! CELEBRATE THANOS!

Zorba certainly sets the stage for our glimpse into the life of this Crystal Valley old-timer. Debby Strom, former general manager of the Redstone Inn, helped organize an evening event with friends and family members in October 2007 to honor Thanos. When we arrived, a small group was clustered in the foyer of the inn around a display of line drawings, paintings and pottery by the Greek-born professor and master of many arts.

The first visit to the Crystal Valley for Thanos was as a hitchhiking teenager in 1942. The story goes that after his stint in the 10th Mountain Division, he came back to Marble in 1945 with a hundred dollars of soldier's muster-out pay, and walked out "a hundred dollars poorer but with a cabin and an acre of land," Thanos used to say.

Longtime friend and Carbondale resident Judy Welch told those gathered that she and her husband Walter had become good friends with Thanos. Their families used to picnic and camp up Lead King Basin together. Her children's favorite story that Thanos told them was about when all the church bells would ring Sunday mornings on the Greek Isles. "We could really hear those bells, Mom!"

Emma Danciger of Carbondale said how she had started a group called "Empty Nesters" in the mid-eighties. During Thanksgiving weekend, each person would bring a dish symbolic of one's childhood holidays and talk about it. His first time, Thanos came in the door, fashionably late of course, in complete Greek costume, bearing a staff and his famous homemade bread. "Needless to say, he stole the day," Emma said, laughing.

At Thanos' Redstone Inn event, more people arrived and began to spill into the lobby of the hotel. Because of so many people, we moved to the adjacent and larger Fireside Lounge. I imagined Thanos looking over us, a big smirk beneath a cloud of white whiskers. I could almost hear Thanos now....

"I'M HERE!"

This boisterous announcement was Thanos' way to say hello. On how Thanos would answer his ringing telephone, Judy and Emma shouted out in unison, "SPEAKING!" Not a bit shy or retiring, some would say Thanos was, well, very confident. Other words to describe him: "complex," "complicated," or how about just "terribly opinionated." Diplomacy was a four-letter word to Thanos....

...AND STUBBORN WAS HIS MIDDLE NAME

One of his neighbors recounted stories about mysterious rocks that would appear overnight in the middle of the road in front of Thanos' house—a Greek speed bump that reappeared after each removal—for years on end.

This writer remembers a grand entrance at one Marble town meeting where Thanos, looking for all the world like Moses down from the mountain with his long, flowing white beard, stomped into the tiny hall, and banged his walking stick on the floor. The roof rose with his bellow, "The Bank stays!" making known his vote on moving the bank building to the local park, a heated political matter du jour.

Joyce Preston, a teacher at the Marble Charter School, shared how much the children during the past several years enjoyed their field trips to see Thanos work in his studio. "He was great with the children," she said. "They loved him." Sometimes it takes a generation or two to connect with progeny.

Thanos was at his winter home in Surprise, Arizona when he had the stroke that stole his life December 2005, but he was laid to rest at the Marble Cemetery. The schoolchildren have written letters to him and tacked them up on the schoolhouse walls after graveside visits, he so impacted their young memories of him. *We miss you, Thanos.*

A gathering of old-timers at Thanos Johnson's home in Marble during late August of 1945. Left to right, they are: Ambrose Williams, Demetra Johnson (holding Demetrious), (bare-chested) Thanos, Mrs. Vanderost (wife of an early ranger in the valley), John Williams and Mr. Vanderost. Courtesy of Oscar McCollum Jr.

"OX-MUSH!"

Back at the party, close friend and traveling cohort Mike Stranahan of nearby Woody Creek perfectly imitated this favorite saying of Thanos'—his way of saying 'Nonsense!' to whatever previous statement was made with which he disagreed. Ox-mush was heard often.

Mike is a great storyteller in his own right. He went on a sentimental journey describing some of his memorable trips with the diminutive Greek iconoclast. "Thanos lived a life full of artistic expression and appreciation of all artistry of a natural way," Mike said.

"COME WITH"

He went on. "One time I arrived with my suitcase for a trip on the Adriatic Coast. Thanos had been invited to visit a countess at her villa and invited me along. He immediately proceeded to direct my repacking. 'This is all you need,' he said, meaning two pairs of pants, three shirts and three sets of underwear. Thanos packed light, in a backpack, ready to go at the drop of a hat. Didn't matter how long the trip; a week or a month, he didn't want a heavy suitcase to slow him down or hold him back.

"Thanos described a lot of amazing things that had happened in his life…and they were all true." said Mike. "Sure, he dramatized once in awhile but he really did some great things that I got to see firsthand." Nothing wrong with a story's perfectly innocent little embellishment here or there, say I.

Mike went on to describe his visit to Korea with Thanos where, once the

Surrounded by happy young hearts, Thanos had to surrender his reputation as curmudgeon.
Courtesy of Marble Charter School

plane landed, they didn't pay for a single thing the entire stay. Thanos was a highly-respected guest to that country. He had documented on behalf of the Smithsonian Institute the works of local potters whose unique craft otherwise would have remained unknown to the world. Those men were now part of the nation's art literati, such as the director of the National Museum.

"SIT!"

Everyone who had ever been a guest at Thanos' home agreed on his great, if not intimidating, hospitality. Thanos would command acquiescence in that voice of deepest *basso profundo*. Then out would come tea, ouzo or Greek coffee and cookies. Guests were treated to his home-cooked meals and Greek specialties that were prepared in a kitchen the size of a coffee table. "He could do amazing things with the simplest ingredients," Emma Danciger said. "But don't step past the line into his kitchen while he was cooking," added Judy Welch.

"Thanos believed that food should be cooked with love and eaten with zest," Mike said.

"That's how he became chef here at the inn in the late forties to early fifties," Debby joined in. "He worked as a dishwasher and stayed in one of the attic rooms. One day the chef quit and the inn owners asked if he would help. He was the chef for seven years before he went off to art school in Cleveland."

The artistry in his famous meals was but one expression of Thanos' celebration of life. Watching him throw pots at his wheel was almost a spiritual experience. This writer found a photo I had taken of Thanos at his hand wheel in 1997. He was contemplating preparations for a ceremonial plate that would be

Above: Thanos in his home gallery. Not only famous for his pottery, Thanos loved to draw pen and ink and watercolor. Courtesy of Marble Charter School

presented at his next trip to Korea that year.

As with food so with clay. Thanos would use the smallest number of ingredients to do the job. "He would take in summer apprentices where he would pay the expenses, the tuition and teach his art," Mike said. Some students reached their own high achievement such as one who went on to apprentice in Korea. Others didn't fare so well under the tutelage of the strict, exacting, but also generous and devoted educator.

"Thanos was a teacher who never stopped teaching," said Mike as he stood and puffed up his chest to get his tenor down to some modicum of Thanos' depth. "He'd say, 'Live each day to the fullest for no day returns.' I can attest that he certainly did.

"I traveled with Thanos on one trip to Korea, six or seven trips to Greece," Mike said. "He could walk my legs off and I'm seventeen years his junior. He was indefatigable!" Mike got a phone call from his old friend a couple days before the fatal stroke.

Let's go to Greece this year, eh, Mike?

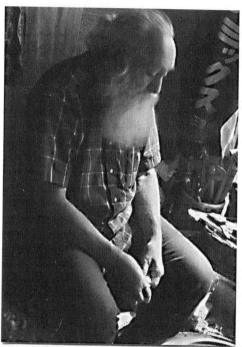

Thanos contemplating preparations for the next ceremonial plate he would take to Korea in 1997. Author photo

" WHY DO ALL THESE WONDER-FUL THINGS HAPPEN TO ME?"

Thanos would often say this when recounting events of his life. There's no question that this Depression-era kid embraced life in Marble with a generous heart.

Chapter 11

ANCESTOR NEWSPAPERS

One of the things I like to do is to peruse area newspapers, especially "freebies" with eye-catching headlines and "Letters to the Editor." Where straight news reporting is (usually) black and white; editorials and columns are the opinion on the subject; colorful, thoughtful, funny, provocative and sometimes sad. They are the "meat on the bone," clothed in individual signature attire. One regular writer in the Aspen papers always signs off, "Be Brave, Comrades." We can count on Ken Moore's' missive to be thought-provoking albeit tongue-in-cheek. Or Carbondale resident, Mildred Baumli's letters, who, in her nineties, has plenty of awareness about current politics and speaks her mind. I hope to do the same when her age.

SMOKE SIGNALS DON'T WORK SO WELL

An ancient stirring in my bones says that historical accounts need to be kept up for future generations. It goes without saying that as a keeper of local history, my file cabinets overfloweth with torn-out editorial pages and copies of newspapers past, not only from "The Big Boys" such as *The Valley Journal, The Aspen Times, Aspen Daily News, Glenwood Post-Independent and High Country News,* but also from the smaller newspapers that have served from Crystal City down through Marble,

Brighter Days for Marble Are in Sight. The End of Our Troubles is Nearing. So, CHEER UP!

THE MARBLE BOOSTER

BY FRANK F. FROST   MARBLE, GUNNISON COUNTY, COLORADO, SATURDAY, AUGUST 26, 1916   VOLUME 6, NUMBER 26

FIRE TAKES HEAVY TOLL

Flames Start in City Drug Store and Destroy Five Business Houses, with Contents, Including Henry Mertens Magnificent Store, U. S. Postoffice and Swigart Building.

FLAMES CHECKED BY GALLO 2-STORY MARBLE BUILDING

Dynamite Used to Blow up Swigart Building, Next to Gallo's, and Heroic Volunteer Firemen Fought the Fire to a Standstill at that Point---Losses Aggregate $35,000.

Fire which broke out at 1:15 o'clock Thursday morning in | the Gallo store, stopping the conflagration at this point. | tion of the town out. Three lines of hose were laid but it

Colorado-Yule Plans for Reorganization

Explained in Detail in Circulars Sent to all Stockholders of Company---Committee Takes Charge of Plans.

J. F. Manning, receiver of the Colorado-Yule Marble company, has sent to this office circulars giving full details of the plan proposed for the reorganization of the company. The reorganization committee is composed of Mortimer Matthews, Norton M. Little and A. J. Mitchell. They are serving without pay.

In reading over the detailed plans by which this committee hopes to protect | new common stock, par value $15, or at said rate.

The proposed new capitalization is as follows:

Bonds and capital stock to be outstanding upon consummation of plans: 6 per cent first mortgage gold bonds (authorized and outstanding) $1,000,000

5 per cent general mortgage gold bonds authorized $1,000,000; outstanding 721,476

5 percent cumulative preferred stock (preferred both as to

The Marble Booster was effusively optimistic about the Colorado Yule quarry… until the Company-controlled newspaper was required, along with town citizens and businesses, to pay damages to his competitor newspaper editor, Sylvia Smith. The marble quarry management refused to pony up. Frustrated, Frost named names and declared there was "…indeed a jinx on the valley."

Redstone on into Carbondale. As we go to press with this Volume 1 of *Memoirs,* already a couple of the papers mentioned above are no more.

These tiny hamlets mostly relied on word-of-mouth, be it the telephone party-line and fliers on mailboxes or bulletin boards between the years of "kitchen-counter newspapers," as I call those smaller publications. Believe it or not, there is a considerable, if not unbelievable, amount of work and dedication that goes into the creation, research, writing, editing and publishing—on a consistent basis—of even the smallest paper. Cranking out my own newsletter, the *Mountain Dweller* by a generator-powered computer and printer at a summer campsite comes to mind.

With few or zero advertisers and zip for staff, most one-person publications usually last a year, maybe three. Thus, there is good reason for acknowledgement and celebration of *The Crystal Valley Echo,* the upper Crystal Valley's monthly paper published by Alyssa Ohnmacht.

"OH, MY GOODNESS, LOOK HOW MUCH YOU'VE GROWN" (groan)

Admit it. Haven't you heard that line at least once in your life—usually from some well-meaning but terribly embarrassing matron? Okay, you found me (except for the matron part; I don't see matron in the mirror).

But such was my double-take when I pulled the December 2007/January 2008 issue of *The Crystal Valley Echo/Marble Times* from my mailbox. The brightly colored headline banner announced "Our Fifth Anniversary" with a full-page photo of Marble Charter School students holding the first issue of the *Echo/Times* with

Alyssa. But, wait. I just saw one of those students during the holidays—a freshman at Harvard University today. Has it really been five years?

Surely, it was only last week that I received Alyssa's call that she was taking over the school's grant-sponsored newsletter we had developed, gosh, back in 2000.

"I plan to make some changes," Alyssa said, "eventually make it a for-profit newspaper including Redstone down to Carbondale." I knew the paper's future was in good hands.

HOW AN ECHO BABY IS BORN, IS BORN, IS BORN

Steve Finn, Marble Charter School's administrator in the late 1990s, had organized both the upper grades upstairs and lower grades downstairs to create a one-page newsletter, in a grandiose sixteen-inch by thirty-inch size. Two of the students wrote a mini-grant request for a new color copier to publish the *Marble Times*, named in honor of the early 1900s Marble Times. Articles were cut-and-paste on the sheet, interspersed with photos of the students. It was sent home once a month, more or less, to let families know the kids' activities in school.

Shortly after, Yours Truly was hired as the steward of a grant awarded to the school. My assignment was to organize a group of volunteers called the Community Leadership Forum (CLF) and together, create a bond between the fledgling charter school and surrounding communities through educational and social endeavors.

The first year of the grant program kicked off with several potluck parties to bring out the social side, movie nights in summer, and a lighted ice rink in winter at the Millsite Park. On the educational side, we planned after-school classes for both children and adults such as astronomy, cooking and yoga. The CLF realized that it didn't do much good to have all these great events if folks didn't know about them. There was no question there were going to be many more events to announce. Reliance on fliers and bulletin boards wasn't going to

"Prosperity, Marble, Colorado" circa 1906, was the supplement of the Glenwood Springs Avalanche newspaper. Marble got plenty of ink for Col. Meek's big plans for the soon-to-be City of Marble. Between two pictures that told the story, jack trains and railroads, "Prosperity" was just over the horizon.

the

MOUNTAIN DWELLER

VOL.01, No10　　　　　　**August, 1998**

A Marble area periodical providing information of interest from Hwy. 133 to Crystal City, CO. for full/part-time residents, business operators, property owners, and interested readers.

"*Leave the Bank where it is!*"

Long, flowing white beard, raised right hand clutching his staff, Thanos A. Johnson, one of the "old-timers" of Marble, looked a lot like Moses coming down from the mountain as he stood before the August 4th Town Council meeting. Once he was acknowledged by the

His remarks were heard by a SRO crowd of area residents, the largest recorded attendance of a council meeting in over two years.

Bettie Lou Gilbert, Vice-president of the Marble Historical Society (MHS) presented a

been a result of several vocal and spirited* meetings (*an endangered action, *see story page 4*) regarding the bank, culminating in the August 1st town public meeting with guest speaker, Gunnison County Manager, John DeVore.

1998: the Mountain Dweller newspaper informs Marble-area public of the meeting that saved the Marble City Sate Bank building from attempts to move the building to the Town's park. Since, as noted in the column, not many people attend town meetings, the Mountain Dweller was one of the "kitchen table" newspapers that evolved to counterbalance political slants of other local papers. This crazy editor? Moi.

be enough. We knew that good communications was critical to success and with a little work, the *The Marble Times* could become that instrument.

Valery Kelly, then a resident of Marble, now Carbondale, became the paper's first editor in 2001. She held classes on newspaper reporting, writing and layout and even organized a field trip to see the operation of *The Aspen Times* offices. She also invited *Aspen Times* veteran writer John Colson to speak at the school about the newspaper "biz" and how to conduct a good interview.

It was amazing to watch and be a part of such focused goodwill and committed involvement of adults—many non-parents—who helped the students grow the *Marble Times* into four to eight pages, folded eleven by seventeen newsletter format. Each month at deadline, volunteer adults would come down to the school, someone would pop some corn, and they would help the students print page after slow-w-w-ly printed page on the copy machine; then fold, staple and sometimes mutilate issues of the infant paper coming "hot off the press" down an animated assembly line.

The grant provided bulk mailings to all households from Highway 133 to the end of County Road 3 at Daniels Hill, plus a growing list of subscribers.

Valery, the students and the CLF reached out to the community. Articles, subscriptions and advertising began to pour in. "It was a great opportunity for the community to have a forum while the kids had a wonderful educational tool to learn about journalism," Valery remembered. "We wanted everyone to know the paper was open to contributions, for everyone to participate, speak their mind."

With these bones, such became the opportunity for the school's paper to become a viable community newspaper. It was ripe for growth. After Valery's

MARBLE TIMES

Volume 1   December 2000

Yellowstone

On Tuesday, September 5, 2000, our 4-8th grade class at the Marble Charter School drove on a 14-hour trip to Yellowstone National Park in Wyoming. We camped out the first night. It was freezing cold and we had to put up all the tents in the dark with only small flashlights to see what we were doing. That night, we heard elk bugling and coyotes howling.

The next day, we saw some of Yellowstone. We saw the famous geyser called Old Faithful. The geyser's water shot up 150 feet into the air. We also saw many other geysers, hot springs, and more. Later that day, we went to the dorms in Mammoth where we stayed for the next three nights.

Yellowstone

Thursday morning, the class went on a hike with a ranger named Sally, who told us some history about the park. Later that night, the class went swimming in a natural hot springs a few miles away from the dorms and then ate Miriam's amazing pizza.

On our last day in Yellowstone, we decided to go to Lamar Valley, a spot where pack of wolves, called the Dru pack, had been sighted on numerous occasions. When we got there, we waited and watched for what seemed hours. After a while, a man

with a telescope spotted the wolves. A very nice couple let our class use their telescope to see them. We got to see the alpha male and female, as we as the other members of the pack, even the pups! After a while, we lost site of the wolves. We went back to the dorms and got ready to leave early the next morning for home. -Laura

|Illustration by Laura Matthews

Marble Charter School

The first Marble Times, December 2000. Big changes came in 2001 with the first adult editor, Valery Kelly, then a resident of Marble, now Carbondale. The novice newspaper became an integral part of the community.

solid start, along came new Marble mom, Alyssa, with her two daughters, to the charter school. Soon the little newsletter took its first determined steps to become the *Echo/Times* of today. The rest, we say, is history. I might add, "…in the making." All agree, Alyssa has done an outstanding job raising this baby.

DOWN THE RABBIT HOLE OF HISTORY WE GO

Should we toss out a rope in case we forget to come back? Oh. That's what deadlines are for, you say? Further research means we crawl into the folds of newspapers past. Carefully we peel open crinkly ambered pages. We're transported back to times long ago. Oh. Look. There is another reporter racing to meet his newspaper deadline. Let's see how that went, one hundred and one years ago.

December 3, 1906. It is another gigantic sixteen by thirty newspaper format with a banner that reads: "Prosperity, Marble Colo." The headline—"Marble's Future."

It states, "Our reporter called on Col. [Channing] Meek, who is president of both the Colorado-Yule Marble Company and the Crystal River & San Juan Railway company, for the purpose of ascertaining the outlook for the future, both of the marble quarries and the railroad."

"Though we have had some difficulties," said Col. Meek, "owing to the rugged character of the country, and perhaps more delays than we anticipated …." He continued his case with optimism gushing like the spectacular Marble waterfalls behind him.

Oscar McCollum's book, *Marble, A Town Built on Dreams, Volume 1,* has excerpts of *Marble Times* and *Crystal Silver Lance* newspapers dated September 1900. The same volume shows a copy of the *Crystal River Current* circa October 1886. Say, isn't this getting to be a familiar trend of names here?

WE'LL TELL YOU WHAT NEWS YOU CAN WRITE

I do have to share a story of one newspaper editor back in the early Marble days, and that is the story of Sylvia Smith, editor of the *Marble City Times* circa 1912, six years after the above Meek interview.

Sylvia was an outspoken liberal and critic of big business. Over to Marble from Crested Butte where she allegedly ran a successful paper, she railed often and loud in her newspaper, the *Marble City Times*. She was the main competitor to Channing Meek's company-controlled *Marble Booster.*

In every issue, Sylvia warned how the company manipulated local business-es and their employees and how she believed it was swindling its investors as well as the quarry employees. She was considered far too radical by business-men who were targets of her attacks, and they were sorely offended when she included articles about women's suffrage in her paper. Oh, no. Don't educate the women. What's the world coming to?

Miss Smith's undoing was her headline that chilly March morning of 1912, after an avalanche crushed the Colorado-Yule Marble Mill: *Destiny kept her Appointment and Redresses many Wrongs.*

It turned out to be the last issue she printed. An impromptu and heated town meeting was held at the behest of the company, presided over by the mayor, an employee of—guess where? He assured everyone that Sylvia was the rotten fish in the barrel. After a show of hands (some claimed coerced), the sheriff put Sylvia in the Marble jailhouse overnight and not so politely escorted her out of town on the train the next day. Her printing press was taken into custody. This headline, "The Marble City Times is Suppressed" was banged out a few days later by the boastful *Booster.*

The ending of this story? Leave it to say that Sylvia redressed a few wrongs herself. The judge granted her some ten thousand dollars (big bucks in those days) in damages and she came back to Marble, this time to collect. History tells us now how after lots of "good faith promises," the company defaulted on their end, leaving townspeople to sell their homes and businesses to satisfy the judg-ment. History also tells us how the *Booster* was the only newspaper in town; that is, until its own ironic end.

Seems the paper's editor had given his final (he thought) word on the Sylvia Smith case. "The *Booster* will be just the same as it always has been—the strongest kind of a 'booster' for Marble, the Colorado-Yule Marble Company and all other industries of the town and vicinity...as far as we are concerned, the dead past is dead." At least that was his position until his newspaper was also targeted by the not-so-dead-after-all Miz Smith.

The fifth anniversary issue of The Crystal Valley Echo and Marble Times since Alyssa Ohnmacht took over as publisher. Alyssa in upper left corner.

BLAME IT ON...OF COURSE, "THE CURSE

In a wire-walking editorial the summer of 1915, the editor "spilled his guts." He chastised the company's position of reneging on promises made before the accidental death of Meek. He alluded to "inside facts" and named names he believed were personally responsible for Sylvia's suit that cost the compromised Marble citizens their homes, if not entire lives' work.

The next reference to the *Booster's* karmic demise was found in the book, *Marble, Colorado, City of Stone* by Duane Vandenbusche and Rex Myers that refers to *Booster* Editor Frank Frost's declaration that he believed "there was indeed a jinx on the valley."

CRAZY ENOUGH TO BE AN EDITOR? UH, WHY?

There doesn't seem to be much available as far as records of old upper valley papers from the early 1900s through the thirties or forties. Of course, that was during the Depression and World Wars I and II. There were references to papers circa 1910 with names like *Marble Age*, "a weekly Republican Newspaper Devoted to the Interests of Marble, Colorado and Colorado Marble."

It was also noted in the *City of Stone* book that the *Marble Meow*, circa 1931, apparently didn't operate very long but was complimented by the Crested Butte paper, the *Elk Mountain Pilot* stating "the *Marble Meow* general staff is to be congratulated on the snappy little paper they put out."

By the early forties, there was no recorded population, at least in Marble, to have need of a newspaper. Oral legends say that after the flood of 1941, three out of the four families in Marble back then didn't much talk to each other anyway. It was joked that one-digit sign language sufficed.

AN ITCH THAT NEEDED SCRATCHING

The next newspaper found was the aforementioned reborn *Crystal River Current,* circa 1970s. The *Current* served the Crystal River valley at ten cents a copy, with distribution to Aspen and Glenwood Springs. I have not yet found when it was discontinued.

When this writer arrived in late 1990s, the *Redstone Reporter* was the upper valley paper, printed twice monthly, in an eleven by seventeen folded newsletter format. It also covered news from Marble. Whether inherent instinct or the fact that I had only recently escaped from the "snake and alligator" world of Big City business, I had an alarming awareness that something fishy was going on in little, ol' quiet Marble. It made the nose itch. Even though the old-timers here warned me repeatedly not to get involved, I ran head-on into "small town politics." Oh, dear.

Ergo; long story short, I created the *Mountain Dweller* in late 1997-'98 during a town election cycle to provide an alternative view of news being reported in the community. What a time...all part of recorded local history too, by the way.

Good, bad or mediocre, there is no doubt newspapers of the present and the past serve a purpose—both to the history and to the future of rural, remote America. They provide the threads that weave stories of communities, their people and events gone by. Whereas today's world news is but a click away, local community news is something to be treasured and will be the resource of future historians such as me. Let us acknowledge the hard work and appreciate the service and dedication of editors all—even if they have to be a little bit crazy.

Chapter 12

EVENTFUL WINTERS PAST - UP THE CRYSTAL

"The first liar doesn't stand a chance," says my dad, Ray. (Of course, dads are right as you'll see below.) We have to shake a leg and get up pretty early for this adventure. We're amongst some real pro storytellers, given the number of Texas transplants that have settled here.

Not that I'm insinuating anything, but let's also pretend we strap on some hip waders under our snowshoes to see how far-fetched we can get in this chapter. And, amongst 'em, I'll do my best to keep all these stories honest. Honest.

STARTING WITH SOME REAL BULL STORIES

For instance, the privileged writer here will start the round with my own astute observation: "Why, we've had so much snow, I swear I saw a bull elk sleeping up in the treetops and," (as any good Texan would add), "I've got pictures to prove it ...somewhere around here."

I am immediately out-storied when I pass the buck to Bill Fender, a long-time Carbondale rancher who, as a kid, spent a lot of time up the Crystal.

"I remember a story about Elmer Bair," he said, "when he delivered mail between Marble and Schofield Pass. He'd snowshoe or cross-country ski back and forth and would tell how he'd sit on the tops of telephone poles to rest." Elmer Bair's name comes up often by storytellers in the Crystal Valley. When it

comes to great tales about the old days, he was one of the most well-known and well-respected pioneers of this area.

When I hear this story, I'm sobered at the realization of the distance—a good eight or nine miles—between Marble and mining camps near Schofield Pass, up in the back country; with absolutely nix, nein, nada, NO kind of help available to the single traveler. And Elmer certainly delivered mail more than once. His fascinating autobiography includes his harrowing experiences during his mail carrier winter job from 1929 to 1930. He took on the mail route "for a hundred and fifty dollars a month" to feed his family when he was temporarily laid off at

Top left, paid $150 a month, Elmer carried mail and supplies between Marble and Ajax mine above Crystal City the winter of 1929-'30. Top right, Otto Schultz, Elmer's brother-in-law; Swan, the boss at the mine; and Elmer at Ajax Mine, located about 14 miles east of Marble. Bottom, The same winter, Elmer Bair, on the far right with his trademark hat, had snowshoes and staff appropriate for his mail route. Courtesy of Bair collection

the Marble quarry. Elmer became well acquainted with what is called the S.O.B. Trail between Crystal and Schofield Park. The trail was aptly named by early miners. A story is told that President Ulysses S. Grant wanted to rename it for a political opponent, "with no loss of meaning" when he traversed Schofield during a hunting expedition in the late 1870s.

CABIN-BOUND CRAZINESS—THE SNOW DEVIL MADE ME DO IT

Avalanche. Whiteouts. Black ice. Power outages. "Mashed-potato" roads—meaning whatever you do, don't stop your car. Interesting stories abound about how people react to one thing man cannot control—weather—and how they deal with the situation in wintertime. Like the one about a crazed writer (uh-oh) rattling around in a remote mountain hotel that, on a snowy night, sure looks a lot like the Redstone Inn (but it's not). And wasn't there one about a nutso nurse that picks up an accident victim on a desolate, icy road? Think Stephen King ever had cabin fever? The fever hits when day after day, temperatures hit subzero and folks can't get out of their homes because snow is blocking their windows, doors and driveways. Grumbles become full-blown arguments. "You're breathing my air!"

It reminds me of a couple stories told by thirty-year Marble resident Joyce Illian. One is a sad story from many years ago about a Redstone Inn employee who headed home during a blizzard one night. She hit a snowbank and died from exposure a few feet from her doorstep, not found until the next day.

"My motto is 'be prepared,'" Joyce said. "Before I leave home, I make sure that I have extra gloves, water, boots to hike a long distance if necessary, and a flashlight."

Joyce remembered the winter of 1983-84 as a year with exceptionally heavy snows. She had bundled up in layers of warm clothing to go shovel a parking spot for her vehicle. The old Joe Manz residence next door was a men's boarding house at the time. With nothing better to do, some of the guys hung out on the deck to make fun of Joyce's hard work. Anyone who has flipped more than a couple shovelfuls in this high altitude sun knows how quickly a sweat can be

Mailboxes huddle under the snow the winter of 1983-84. Courtesy of the Kimbrell Family Collection

"This is how short people move the snow," says 85-year-old Shirley Thomson as she pitches a shovelful over her shoulder. "There is nowhere else to put it." Shirley and David moved to Redstone fulltime in 1979 so she has had plenty of practice. "You learn to cope."

worked up. Little by little the clothing layers peeled off until Joyce was down to her sports bra. "The guys kept joking and laughing," she said.

Pretty soon, one fellow came home, backed into the driveway up against the snowbank, and knocked a huge pile of snow right back into the cleared space. Joyce yelled in frustration. The peanut gallery erupted. Her husband, Ronnie, came to her rescue. He charged over the snowpile to duke it out with the first fella he saw. As they parried punches, this tiny, half-dressed woman climbed up over the five-foot bank, shovel in hand, intent on breaking up the brawl. Instead of busted lips, they all busted up laughing at the scene they created. "It pays to have a sense of humor," Joyce said, chuckling.

DEAR SANTA, ALL WE WANT FOR CHRISTMAS

Pat and Hank Kimbrell, former owners of Beaver Lake Lodge in Marble, also remembered the same winter.

"It began on November 19, 1983," Pat said, "It snowed for forty days straight. I remember the day it started because I had gone to Aspen to pick up my oldest son flying in from Florida. It was bluebird weather. I was in a flannel shirt. The next day, it started to snow and didn't stop until after the first of the [new] year.

"John Darien cleared the road in those days," she continued. He lived in the county shop, [now the restored Marble City State Bank building]. The snow got so high, we couldn't see other cars coming around the corners so folks put orange balls on the tips of their car antennas, hoping others would see them coming. Eventually, the county brought over some big equipment to cut the snowbanks down."

Hank remembered how, during that winter, so much snow slid off the roof that it created a tunnel alongside the lodge. He said their kids would jump off the front balcony deck and onto the snowbank to wait for the school bus.

"Our four kids grew up at the lodge and slept in the attic," Pat said. "Of course, it wasn't insulated back then and in the winter, they would get up in the morning and the water in the glasses by their bedside had frozen. The blessing of those days was that with no television or radio, the kids didn't know to ask for the advertised toys at Christmastime. They all asked for and got electric blankets."

And speaking of frozen water, this writer remembers a story by Shaunlee and Spike Blaine, who now live in Hawaii. No wonder. They told us of how they lived in a yellow school bus one winter while building their cabin. Shaunlee said their dog went to lick water that had spilled from his bowl and his tongue got stuck on the metal floor. Are we shivering yet?

ANY OL' STORK IN THE STORM WILL DO

The next record snow year was 1992-1993. Patsy Wagner, owner of the Inn at Raspberry Ridge, especially remembered that winter. "Our neighbors, Miriam and Bob Leone, who owned the Crystal River Way Station, [the former Mountain View Inn] planned a home birth for their second child," Patsy said. "I admired how strong a woman Miriam was to do that."

They had asked Patsy earlier on if, when it was time, she would come over to be with and explain the process of the baby's birth to their 2-year-old daughter, Abbey.

"It was February 1993, in the middle of a storm," remembered Patsy, "Miriam went into labor. It was snowing so hard, we were concerned that the midwife couldn't make it up to Marble, but both parents handled it very well. They had candles lit and soft music playing in the background."

When we talked to Miriam, she told us that the midwife made it in time but that Bob was still pretty nervous. "Mir" was very matter-of-fact about the occasion. "Yes, it was pretty laid-back," she said. "I squatted and everyone helped." Within a half hour, Miriam invited neighbors over to see the baby. (You go, girl.) Then she shared how the day I called about this story was coincidentally their son's fifteenth birthday. They had been reminiscing about that winter. Today, Luke (guess we can't call him Lukey anymore) is a football and rugby player and has been recently awarded junior poet laureate at his school.

SKI FIRST...THEN GET YOUR PRIORITIES STRAIGHT

Clark Heckert from Delaware, with a second home across from the old Placita townsite, remembered that same winter in his own exciting way (men!).

"I was building my cabin then," Clark said. "In early December, instead of getting the heat in first, I was so excited to ski that I scratched up my new skis on the rocks. When I came out again in January, there was five feet of snow and all this great powder, but I had to get my priorities in order. I ended up carrying my heating materials from the highway to the cabin using my old L.L. Bean snowshoes. Even then, I was post-holing my way in."

Indeed, it takes tough people to live in tough country. This certainly isn't a place for whiners with entitlement issues. That neighbor you righteously cussed one day may be the only one around to pull you out of the river the next.

Chapter 13

HEARTBREAK HOTEL—
CRYSTAL VALLEY MANOR

The year is 1956. Ponytails and poodle skirts. Ducktails and blue suede shoes. Even Marble had heard of Elvis Presley. The rock and roll king's first million-record hit song, "Heartbreak Hotel" had blasted off the charts.

"WELL, SINCE MY BABY LEFT ME, (ta-dum)
I'VE FOUND A NEW PLACE TO DWELL (ta-dum)"

Meanwhile, Wade and Wilma Loudermilk had built the Beaver Lake Lodge. Readers will remember from the Marble Memorial Airport story, that Wade had all the right excavating equipment to build the airstrip. The family would come up from the Phoenix area to escape the summer's heat. They rented out horses and guided Jeep tours besides housing and feeding their guests.

Business was running at a good clip when they began to host annual visits for Baylor University's Summer Geological Field Course groups. There just so happened to be a male majority of the thirty to thirty-five students in attendance from early June through mid-July; the odds of which did not go unnoticed by the Loudermilk daughters—college-aged Raquel and her high-school sister, Kareen. Pretty much the only two girls in Marble at the time, they decided to

Heartbreak Hotel 1958. "No Vacancy" permanently scripted on the sign tells this story. Courtesy of Ben and Kareen Man Collection.

share their summer social largesse with Raquel's USC sorority sister, Ann Smith. They invited her to come to work with them.

"We were the slave-labor force," said Kareen. "It was a lot of hard work but we didn't mind. We had a lot of fun."

SURE THERE'S ROOM, YOU'RE SKINNY!

Beds in the lodge and its cabins were stacked to the rafters and they still ran out of room. They had another cabin down towards the Crystal River across from the old Marble jailhouse and their horse stables. It isn't clear if they sometimes used the pokie and paddocks too. But, even that wasn't enough.

The Loudermilks then rented a small cabin east across the road from the lodge. None of the accommodations had running water or indoor toilets. Rows of metal bunkbeds were the only adornments.

Ann was quite the artist, so she painted a sign to put over the door of the cabin closest to the lodge, thusly christened "Heartbreak Hotel." Later on, folks would arrive at the lodge and ask to be booked next door at the Heartbreak. They really thought it was a hotel. Those poor fellows stuck down at the decidedly unromantic cabin next to the horse stables felt left out and pouted. So Ann penned another sign for them: "Leper Colony."

"We eventually had to take the 'Leper Colony' sign down as it scared the tourists," Kareen told us, "but we got a lot of mileage on the jokes about both places."

"and though it's always crowded,
you still can find some room,
for brokenhearted lovers
to cry there in the gloom."

DEAR JOHN…and JOE, FRED, and TOM

It became a common event those summers that the postman would leave "Dear John" letters at the lodge for the boys staying there. After all, in teen time, June to July was oh, so long.

"The bell hop's tears keep flowing,
the desk clerk's dressed in black."

"We would have big bonfires every night," Kareen said. "That was our entertainment in those days. There would be a guy with a guitar and we would sing songs. 'Heartbreak Hotel' was a popular request. I remember one lovesick guy who was a newlywed. He wouldn't change his watch from Waco time where his bride was."

While Raquel and Ann played the field, Kareen caught the eye of one young man named Ben. Ben Man was a third-year geology student that summer of '56. Spurred by the competition, it took Ben nearly three years of long-distance letter-writing and courting before the couple became engaged over Christmas of '58 in Marble. They wed at the Marble church the following October.

"I had always wanted a fall wedding up here," said Kareen. "Turned out it was the earliest snowstorm in history that October third. Our best man and minister were stuck on Loveland Pass due to the snow. They did finally arrive and I've never heard the end of it about my wanting a fall wedding." As we go to press, we learn there are plans for a fiftieth wedding anniversary celebration in Marble come October '09.

SO IF YOUR BABY LEAVES YOU…THERE'S A PLACE TO DWELL

Actually, I first heard about Heartbreak Hotel by the delightful storyteller and lifetime Marble resident June Blue in 1997. It was certainly an honor to meet itty-bitty June with the waist-long silver hair. The Blue family home was, and still is, adjacent to Thanos Johnson's place and across the road from the little cabin with the broken-hearted reputation.

June told me during a visit with her one time that, "every spring, there was a lot of activity over there, like musical chairs, people moving out, others moving in… winters here are long… and tiring! The losers ended up at Heartbreak Hotel."

THE BEAT GOES ON

By the early seventies, the cabin was absentee-owned and suffered the indignities of neglect. Occasionally, bargain-priced paint would be slapped on, such as the time it was covered with highway-stripe-reflective-yellow. It glowed in the dark. Made it much easier for inebriates to find their way home at night, I'm told. Alas, for years and years, it sat lonely, abandoned and forlorn.

That is, until one day far away in another location, three girlfriends, tired of the desert hippie scene, made a life-changing decision. Patty Vanderhoof, niece of John D., the former governor of Colorado, told her best friends, Sue and Marilyn,

"Hey, I have a friend who has a cabin up in the mountains. Let's go there!"

Not long after they arrived, Marilyn bailed. June's son, Kirk, along with the handful of other hardened year-round locals, watched with an interested eye as the remaining two girls adapted to their first winter of mountain life.

"There was only an outhouse and they still had to carry water from Carbonate Creek," Kirk said. "Marge Orlosky [quite the mountain woman herself] and all of us had bets on how long they would survive." Kirk added with a chuckle, "I gave them the longest—two months." But Kirk and Company didn't realize how bull-headed the blond-haired beauty named Sue and her friend were. He had to take another look.

YOUR WOOD SMELLS FUNNY

Sue told me how it got "so-o-o cold, forty below zero for at least ten days," that she and Patty would bring in the outhouse toilet seat at night to keep it somewhat warmer. The bummer was that many times in the morning they would forget to take it back outside. So they got to using a chamber pot. One night a chimney fire started. The girls had nothing to throw on it but the filled pot. They didn't get around to telling Kirk that information when he came to help clean out the stove and chimney the next day.

THE MAN WITH ALL THE TOYS...WINS

Sue and Patty both got jobs at the Redstone Inn, which is almost a rite of passage for locals—Patty as a waitress, Sue as a dishwasher. Sue's "waste not, want not" philosophy took offense when she saw the amount of leftover food being tossed out in the kitchen. She took it all home. Just like in the natural world, it didn't take long for the free food source to be found. Pretty soon, all manner of wild and woolly mountain characters came out of their hidey-holes to chow down at the Heartbreak.

While the other "pockets-empty" fellas made their lovelorn pitches, there was one neighbor who always had the chainsaw, the washing machine, the hot water showers—all the conveniences the girls might need. "That would be me," said Kirk, grinning. Looks like it paid off. Kirk and Sue Blue have been married coming up on thirty years.

A LEGEND WAITS IN THE WINGS

Heartbreak Hotel has a new owner and like other ladies of a certain age, has had a flattering facelift. Now a sparkling bride-white paint job dresses up new windows, roof and porch but, alas, there are no new tales to tell. I'll watch and await the next chapter of this legend.

REDSTONE'S CRYSTAL VALLEY MANOR

There was nothing like a well-placed newspaper ad in the July 1973 issue of the *Crystal River Current* to remind folks that there were other places to stay along the Crystal. Fishing at Redstone was and still is world class. In fact, there's a certain fishing contest that serves up an interesting hook in this next story.

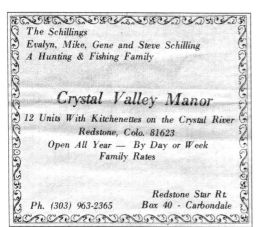

The Schillings
Evalyn, Mike, Gene and Steve Schilling
A Hunting & Fishing Family

Crystal Valley Manor

12 Units With Kitchenettes on the Crystal River
Redstone, Colo. 81623
Open All Year — By Day or Week
Family Rates

Ph. (303) 963-2365   Redstone Star Rt.
Box 40 - Carbondale

Let's mosey on down the river and check out the Crystal Valley Manor.

Mike Schilling is the former owner of Redstone Stables and Avalanche Outfitters. The Schilling family also owned the Crystal Valley Manor motel, built in 1962-'63 by Mike's parents, Ed and Evalyn. Since 1977, Mike and his wife, Judy have lived north of Redstone in the Janeway subdivision of the Crystal Valley.

The Crystal Valley Manor is about a third of the way down Redstone Boulevard, next to the Church at Redstone. The L-shaped motel sits on the river and beautifully sculpted gardens grace the motor court entrance come summertime.

NEVER MET A FISH HE DIDN'T WANT TO CATCH

Originally from Scotts Bluff, Nebraska, how did the Schillings find Redstone?

"Our family was really into fishing first and foremost," Mike said. "We were living in Aurora at the time and so we'd fish the Granby/Walden area. Dad would read in *The Denver Post* newspaper about the Dave Cook Fishing Contests that were held weekly on selected Colorado rivers back then. We kept hearing how fishermen on the Roaring Fork were winning all the time." In those days, Mike said the prizes were big and impressive. "Seems someone fishing there would win a boat nearly every week," he said.

To this day, Mike fondly remembers when a perfect "day in the life" consisted of Dad and first son out wettin' a line. One Sunday, Evalyn took the Schillings' bored little brothers, Gene and Steve, on a drive up a dirt road. She came back raving about a place they had found called Redstone. The family returned to check it out. "We all flipped out," Mike said. Next thing they knew, it was on a Valentine's Day that they bought the land they fell in love with and where their manor would sit.

NOT SHARING STRAWS ANYMORE

Mike said that his two younger brothers missed out on most of the building of the motel. "I was only twelve years old," Mike said. "It was spring break in 1962 that we came out to lay the foundation. There were no cement trucks delivering those days. Mom worked the cement mixer, so tired and sore she was crying, but she didn't stop. She knew we had to finish up."

Young Mike caught on real quick how to fill in and smooth the concrete surface, all hundred-some yards of footers for the motel. "At the end of the day, I was whipped and I remember how Dad said he would get me anything I wanted as a reward for a good job," he said. "Back then, I always had to share whatever we got with my two brothers so I told him, 'I want a bottle of Coke all by myself.'"

The family came back that summer and worked until their money ran out. They lost prime building time while they had to wait for a Small Business Association loan to go through. When it finally did, school was starting up again. They decided Mike would stay and work with his dad. He enrolled in Carbondale's seventh grade class while Mom took the younger boys back to Aurora. "I became more of a man, less of a kid that year," said Mike.

"After school, I'd work with Dad and then cook us dinner," Mike said. "We ate a lot of cube steak and fried taters." Mike also remembered how one winter night he heard a scratching at the door. He opened it to find a shivering stray dog he'd seen hanging around. He took it in. Good thing. That night the temperatures dipped to minus forty-two degrees. Mike and his dad kept a hatchet by the cabin's door to chop the ice off the door to get out in the morning. Needless to say, that was one grateful dog. He was named "Poochie Pounder" or "Poochie" for short.

A REAL GRAND DAME SLEPT HERE

A junior-high school student at the time, Mike especially remembered there was one guest that often stayed at the manor. He didn't think much of it at the time, but she loved to tell the young boy stories about her "good old days." Her name was Lucille McDonald, the third and last wife of the founder of Redstone, John Cleveland Osgood.

"I wish I had had a tape recorder then," he said. "She told all kinds of stories I've forgotten over time." (Aha, writers—we're reminded the reason for our existence.)

Other return guests that were some of Mike's favorites were John and Mary Terry from Houston, Texas. "He was the most jovial, fun-loving person," Mike said. "He loved fish frys. In fact, he had special thirty-inch pans made up. He'd fry up fish and a big ol' mess of potatoes. He wouldn't even be unpacked from the car before he'd call all us kids around. He told us he would give us a dime or quarter for every fish we caught. Be sure to get in your story that I caught lots more fish than my two brothers," Mike added.

With baby brother Steve now in Hawaii, and middle brother Police Chief Gene busy keeping the peace in Carbondale, I'll just stay up here knowing I can take Mike's word for it. Ya think?

PEPE LE PEU WALTZES IN

One scented memory that stands out to Mike was the year of the skunks. And this was no Chinese calendar event that winter of 1965-'66. No one dared step foot outside after dark. Seems the black and white kitties had a nightly fashion parade up and down the Boulevard…that is until resident Larry Campbell had his dogs sprayed one too many times.

Larry launched a counter-offensive attack, charging up and down the

Best wishes from our family to yours

The Ed Schilling's

The Schilling Family's Christmas card early 1960s. Courtesy of Schilling family.

Boulevard in his open-top Jeep. The moonlit snow made for easy targets. All night, everyone in town could hear the boom, boom, boom of his guns. No one complained. The next morning, kids counted up. *Looky here! Gotta be a hundred skunks ol' man Campbell kill't and stuffed in this gunnysack.*

The second night he bagged another seventy or eighty of the stinkers. By the end of Campbell's Crusade, more than two hundred skunks weren't a'waltzing down the Boulevard any more. Mike said they must have gotten the message. The skunks have not returned en masse like that since.

HOOK, LINE AND SINKER

By 1968, Mike got his first real summer job, meaning he actually got paid a wage to work for the Forest Service trail crew. There he met Kaye Donne Ferguson, son of Mary and Jack. Kaye Donne taught Mike about horses and cattle and they became good friends. They didn't know then how intertwined their lives really were.

"Some years later, we were talking one day when something came up about Dave Cook's fishing contests being what got us up here," said Mike. He found out that Kaye Donne and friends were the ones catching all the record-winning fish from the Roaring Fork river he'd heard about.

"Then he tells me that they were catching these twelve to fifteen pounders—not in the Roaring Fork after all—but in …(*ahem*) another secret location." *Yes, Mike. Go on. My brother David will love me for this insider info.*

Anyhow, turns out the guy winning all the boats and prizes in the fishing contests some fifteen years earlier—that had grabbed Mike and family hook, line and sinker—ended up being Best Man in Mike's wedding in January 1977. Go figure.

Chapter 14

AN ANGEL FROM HEAVEN IN MARBLE—
BLEU STROUD

As far as I'm concerned, this Crystal valley is as close to Heaven as one can get without checking in. A beautiful lady named Bleu Stroud, who hailed from Nebraska, lived in Marble for some thirty years from the nineteen sixties to early nineties. In 2008, Bleu checked in—from and back to the most beautiful valley of all.

I feel most fortunate to have been touched by Bleu's ageless spirit. I've collected herein snippets by friends and family but all agree that we're barely scratching the surface. And how do we describe Bleu?

OUR LAST HELLO

I last got to visit with Bleu in August 2007 at her home in Black Forest, outside Colorado Springs. She had moved there from Marble in 2000.

Bleu was casually dressed in navy slacks and a robin egg blue sweater, emphasizing her clear blue eyes and her signature kerchief around her neck. Bright red lipstick was fresh on full, cupid lips, signature blond curls now lined in silver, still reminiscent of the Vargas models of the World War II era. Most striking, however, was the fair, china-bisque clear complexion of this still-beautiful lady. There was no way to know then, but Bleu had just turned ninety.

Her son Paul Stroud shared circa-1920 photos of Lil' Miss Bleu. You can see her sense of humor was already defined with her creative adornment of oatmeal boxes. Watch out world!

BETTER'N BETTY GRABLE

Bleu certainly looked like a World War II pinup girl, but as a young woman, her beauty was more of a handicap and her military life much less glamorous, if not down-right dirty. Bleu was the only female mechanic of B-17s during wartime. As it turns out, Bleu was somewhat famous during the war but rather than for her ruby red lips, it was for her pants. Yes, you read right. Pants. Bleu was in the Womens Air Corp (WAC) and became the first female airplane mechanic. As such, her WAC skirt wasn't the least bit practical atop the scaffolding of the airplanes she repaired.

"I had learned mechanics from my father and brothers and for me to do something (during wartime) that I could do well only made sense to me," said Bleu. After going toe to toe with her superiors, she was able to get special dispensation to do the practical thing and wear pants on the job.

EMERALD, THE BROTHER, NOT THE CITY...

...is how Bleu first heard of Marble. Her brother was a photographer who sent color slides of the area to his sister during the fifties. In the early sixties, she and husband, Howard, moved to Marble from California. The Strouds first purchased one acreage, and then other, then another—accumulating something more than thirteen hundred acres at one point in time. In those days, large amassings of land were easy. Numerous lots and mines in this upper valley had been abandoned by the late forties and could be picked up for delinquent taxes.

Little Miss Bleu - a beauty with a sense of humor even as a child. Courtesy of Stroud Collection

While Howard tended to business, Bleu shared her passion for the arts in Glenwood Springs where she was an art teacher at Colorado Mountain College (CMC) from its early days and also involved with the Glenwood Springs Art Guild for many years. I constantly run into ladies who took Bleu's art classes.

After a divorce, Bleu's solitary year-round life in the most remote and rugged part of the upper Crystal Valley of the sixties and seventies was extremely harsh, particularly for such a beautiful, talented, tenacious, single woman. She told me how she learned so much about the area's backcountry. With only her small dog and a rifle, Bleu would be sent off by outback guides to circle around the Gallos Mountains north of Marble to flush out elk and deer toward the hunters. As successful shots rang out, Bleu would swing back around to camp and have a full-course breakfast prepared for their return, with never a thought to the cliff-hanging dangers she had just skirted.

She and another of her tail-wagging partners would hike overnight beyond the Marble Falls with nothing but a string hammock shoved in her pocket and a penknife to hunt for mushrooms. Imagine the shock to find out, that in physical age, Bleu was more than eighty years old before she slowed down those hikes. You see, whether with a canvas and brush or a chainsaw in hand, Bleu was ever the elegant lady. One just didn't ask her age. Bleu was indeed ageless.

Having climbed the Mount of Sixty Years, this writer is a new sexagenarian, even if I can't pronounce it. And, as much as I'd like to think of myself as an adventurous soul, I'm thinking there is NO way I could sleep outside in this big, BIG backcountry world all by myself with nothing but the company of a small, albeit loyal, dog…and nada but a wad of string between me and terra firma. HA! Dream on, unless, of course, we adopt a Bleu attitude.

PATHWAY TO HEAVEN

Bleu was totally connected with the earth, nature and her surroundings. Even as she aged, she explored the great outdoors with free abandon. There was never a word about how "old" she got.

Bleu was a friend to every one of God's creatures she met on her path. This is not a story the Colorado Department of Wildlife people want to hear but there are many stories about Bleu's motherly attention to feed one and all—the fox, deer, elk and bear. She even raised one baby deer in her home. She described it to me as "an articulated bunch of sticks." The baby deer named Schachie learned to run down the drive and bark with all the other dogs as Bleu drove out her driveway.

SINGING IN THE RAIN

1961—Bleu sits in her home, the Marble Falls outside her window. Courtesy of Stoud collection

Bleu stoically faced down political attacks against her because of the controversial Marble Ski Area days of the early seventies and the potential development of the land she then owned. She endured gossip, innuendo and childish pranks by a few not-so-nice neighbors. "Little did they know, I had plenty of experience with that in the military," Bleu said ruefully.

It turned out that politics du jour were instrumental in Bleu's decision to leave the valley in 1999. The most difficult of Mother Nature's actions she could endure. People's politics she could not. It is certain that in her creative artist's heart, there was no room for such negativity. Plus there were other considerations at the time. She wanted to move closer to family and care for a sick friend. And in Black Forest, she found another home with acreage to spread her artistic flair. Soon a wily red fox, squirrels and others became her new best four-legged friends. All these and other stories Bleu shared during that August visit. We found another coincidence to our kinship—our birthdays were one day apart. We made plans to meet in the spring to visit again.

POWER OF POSITIVE THINKING

We all know this saying, but do we really understand the magnitude of positive thinking? Bleu did. She knew she had cancer for a number of years but never, ever, told anyone. She self-treated with homeopathies and a careful diet and chose never to give it a voice. Bleu refused to succumb to the obvious negative diagnoses and implications. However, Bleu did voice her distain for conventional drug treatments. A glance around her home and it was obvious that she was well-read and current on numerous cancer and other disease-related subjects.

Bleu was knowledgeable about every healing herb in the mountains she loved. She was as close to an Indian medicine woman as any non-Indian could be. Who knows. Maybe she was. She was very aware and very respectful of Ute history and spirits. In her writings and her paintings she spoke their language of love with Nature in its most natural way.

IF I HAD IT TO DO OVER AGAIN

Well, c'mon. Amongst the over-the-hill gang, it IS the silent question most asked in the mirror, right? For Bleu, it was damn the tongue-wagging torpedoes. Bleu lived her life her way, a true testament to the power of positive thinking.

Judy Welch of Carbondale shared some of her memories of Bleu going back over forty years ago.

"I remember Bleu as the original mountain woman—at least in my mind. She hunted and fished and rode horseback, Jeeped and sewed, painted —walls AND pictures—and cooked! She had the most beautiful skin/complexion of any woman I knew and know. Her secret? Vaseline.

"Bleu and I shared books, meals, rummage sales, late night talks in front of the fire, and our own memories. I heard all about her 'ferrying' airplanes, her trips in the modified RV to Alaska—trips back and forth to see the family in Nebraska.

"Bleu was a special friend and my memories of her and our times together are something really special. I'm glad that I have each and every one of them...with an occasional tear or two to wipe away."

MARBLE TO BLACK FOREST

Nancy Kujak of Floresville, Texas was a neighbor after Bleu moved from Marble to Black Forest around 1999. Nancy is also a retired female in the military. She related to Bleu's stories told about life as a WAC during World War II.

"Bleu paved the way for future generations of women to have the opportunities to serve in almost any career in the military—I am one of those who benefited from her paving the way," said Nancy.

"She followed the golden rule and treated people with dignity and respect. She had ethics and manners and grace. She followed the laws, was humane, helped her neighbors and helped others. She had a great work ethic and energy for days.

"With Miss Bleu, you could not separate nature and her—it would be like trying to ski without snow or swim without water. She would not have been happy in a cookie cutter

Bleu with son Paul Stroud when he retired from the U.S. Air Force after 22-plus years . Paul followed his mother's footsteps as an aircraft mechanic. Courtesy of Stoud collection house in a cookie cutter neighborhood. She needed space to be herself, to spread her wings and be free."

Duncan Sinnock of Glenwood Springs shared these memories:

"My family had moved to Redstone in the fall of 1967 and I soon became friends with (Bleu's son) Paul Stroud. Bleu took me under her wing, letting me join them for endless weekends and entire summers of adventures. Oh, believe me, each and every moment with Bleu was an adventure.

"Bleu was the only year-round resident in Marble back then. She would wake us for school at 5:00 a.m. while she had risen at 3:45 a. m. herself and plowed the road from [her home] the Snowshoe Ranch all the way to the bottom of McClure Pass where we would meet the school bus at 6:00 a.m. There were always sour dough pancakes and warm hot chocolate for breakfast. Bleu is the only person I have ever met with a 17-year-old batch of sour dough pancake mix and man, they were good.

"I remember Bleu moving a large group of low-life drifters from her gold mine with a .38-caliber in 1968. We went to the mine to camp and came upon these drifters. Bleu, while resting her hand on the butt of the gun at her hip, spoke in a calm tone. 'That's fine, you go on and finish your pumpkin soup and be on your way.' Never giving an actual threat and never saying 'if you don't , I'll'...then she eased the whole group on down the mountain while finishing in a smooth voice, 'The place at the bottom is mine too, so keep on going.'

"I drove to her home in Colorado Springs the week before her passing. I had not seen Bleu or Paul in over thirty years. We sat and talked of those wonderful memories, the fun and laughter we all cherished in our Marble days. My wife was amazed that all the movie-like adventure stories were in fact true. My time with Paul in Marble as a young boy was wonderful and precious and all possible because of a woman named Bleu, the Queen of Marble."

THE TREASURY MEN ARE COMIN'

Bleu said certain friends came every summer to camp out at the same gold mine she owned up on Sheep Mountain that Duncan mentioned. I got to meet them the summer of '08 when they came with Paul to honor and spread Bleu's ashes.

After just a few minutes, I could see why Bleu looked forward to their annual arrival. What a hoot. Federal Customs agents, state and city police by profession—these retired gentlemen and their sons, and now grandsons, were resting up after another hard day in mountain paradise…fishing, eating, drinking, fishing, napping, storytelling and fishing. We can see why they needed the rest. Fly fishing is hard on the beer-holding wrist.

A MARVELOUS LADY

When it came to talking about favorite Bleu memories, these gentlemen were all talking at once, so I can't name them each here. But all of their memories were full of good times.

"We're from all over—Texas, Arizona, Maryland. We even have a Yokie in the group (a Yankee living in Oklahoma), " said one.

"Bleu took us under her wing in 1976. She let us camp on her property in front of the waterfalls for four years before she sold it. They let us stay one summer and then Bleu offered this site in 1980."

"Cuz we made too much noise!" (No doubt.)

"Bleu was a great cook. She would pick wild mushrooms and make wonderful dishes. I remember her spaghetti," said another. "And her chokecherry jelly!" said one more.

"Remember how she taught Bill Hughes and Duke Smith how to hunt elk that one year?"

"I remember the horseshoe pitching tournaments she had at her house."

"She would come to visit and walk all the way up Daniels Hill. When we'd offer to drive her back down, she'd tell us no, she wanted the exercise. Found out she was eighty then. We never knew her age. She was older than any of us. You'd never know it."

BLEU NOTES ON THE LEFT BANK

As much as she loved her many summer visitors, Bleu's own reminisces told the hostess's side of the story when published during the mid-seventies in the "Crystal River Current," a local newspaper back then.

This is the time of year when we weary natives get restless to go camping for some respite from people who camp with us, and other summertime frenetics. Any day now, something will snap and off we will sneak, each to his own little laughing place somewhere out there to retrieve our sanity and replenish our souls.

"...armed with my little dog, Si, who won't leave the Jeep for more than five minutes, a tin of smoked oysters, crackers and a thimble of cherry wine, I set out to confer with nature on an eyeball-to eyeball basis. Ten hours later, I had crawled through enough waist-deep grass and wildflowers to ferret out a marketbag full of Boletus and Velvet Stemmed Collybia Mushrooms, a hill of biting mad ants and two water snakes. From the old Chidester Homestead area, I brought back a small fistful of columbine, for painting, clumps of daisies and horsemint, for transplanting, and a bunch of mixed wildflowers for the Sunday Church service....plus sufficient euphrasy to carry me through another few days. Acres of glistening white daisies have taken over the old horse pastures up there, transforming them into arenas of pristine, new fallen snow in the middle of surrounding lush greenery. Enough to make one kick off the hiking boots and otherwise take leave of the senses. Every time I'm sure that the mountains couldn't be more beautiful than at this instant, they become so. God bless

ON THE WINGS OF LOVE SHE GOES

Nancy Kujak shared an eloquent tribute to Bleu:

In life and in death Miss Bleu was elegant and grand. She was positive, motivating and poised. She chose to share her struggles only with the universe and nature.

She asked me within weeks before she left, "Nancy, why do you suppose hundreds and hundreds of birds flocked to my home ... as of late?" At the time, I did not know the answer, but I do now. The answer is that they came along with the whole of nature to carry her home!

Bleu with one of her four-legged children. Photo courtesy of Meredith Ogilby, from her book, "Women of the Roaring Fork."

Chapter 15

SHIRLEY AND DAVID THOMSON—
24 CARAT GOLD PILLARS IN THE
"RUBY OF THE ROCKIES"

The long and the short of this story is David at six foot-four and Shirley tip-toeing to scrape the five foot mark. How did they ever see eye to eye? Yet for sixty-two "and a fraction" years of marriage, they did just that, before David "graduated," as Shirley calls his passing in August of 2004.

SPEEDY SNEAKERS REQUIRED
I had to put on my fastest sneakers to catch up with Shirley Thomson. After all, at eighty-some years young, she has no intention of letting age dictate her itineraries. If she isn't at the Hot Springs Pool in Glenwood Springs doing her requisite half-mile swim a couple times every week, Shirley is punching numbers on an adding machine and taking care of the treasury for the Marble Community Church, the Redstone Art Center, and Redstone Community Association (RCA) and other area business clients. And she works for these

Wedding Day, June 1942. The tall and short couple saw eye-to-eye for sixty-two and a "fraction" years before David 'graduated," as Shirley calls his passing in 2004. Well, except for the "honey-moon-blanket" incident. Courtesy of the Thomson Collection

businesses and folks between day-trips with good friends or solo junkets to see family. As with a number of other local "energizer bunny" elders I've met, something crystal-clear is Shirley's attitude about "old age." Up here, one almost never hears, "I'm too old and can't…."

Shirley and I visited in her cozy, warm dining room on the boulevard in Redstone where, on this particular occasion, we managed to at least see out through the top half of a heavily snow-banked bay window. Over tea, we laughed at the antics at her feeders in front of a north view of Mount Sopris. We were being entertained by a cacophony of birds—junkos, two or three kinds of chickadees, three kinds of nuthatches, bright yellow finches, evening grosbeaks, and woodpeckers.

In her backyard Steller jays strutted in their bright blue tux n' tails on thin, bright red western dogwood stems and pecked away at Shirley's suet-concocted ornaments. She said how the Roaring Fork Audubon Society makes a point of annual bird observations at her feeders. They've told her that she has the most variety of birds in the entire valley.

NOT WITH MY NEW BLANKETS!

"So, how long have you been looking out this window, Shirley?"

"We moved here full-time in the spring of 1979." Shirley replied. "We were living in Marshalltown, Iowa and we had been coming out and camping between the Frying Pan and Crystal rivers since the fifties."

Shirley said how since their marriage in 1942, she knew that life with David Thomson would not be static. In fact, she learned a lot about David that first month of marital bliss.

"We were married in June and had two days off for a honeymoon, which we took in Maine," she said. "David worked in Massachusetts for the Civil Service on the B-17s that flew over England during World War II. He worked seven days on, one day off. He would eventually get two days off in a row and as a new bride, I was really counting on that first two-day weekend as husband and wife. Turned out I was counting on one thing and he was counting on another. He came home and said, 'We're going on a camping trip (with his Boy Scout Troop).'"

The new bride responded as only a new bride would: "I'm sorry! You're not taking any of my new blankets!" In those days, there were no sleeping bags. Bedrolls were made of blankets only, Shirley explained.

David took off camping with his scouts—sans bride or blankets. Shirley took up doghouse building. Just kidding.

PUT THAT ADDRESS IN PENCIL, PLEASE

Somewhere in their engagement, David told Shirley, "We're not buying a house unless it is in Colorado." Shirley must have learned to pack light. Having met at church in New Jersey, they lived in North Carolina, Iowa, Kansas, Texas and Lima, Peru. (*Whew!*)

Next stop: Pueblo, Colorado. David was hired as an instructor at Pueblo Junior College and soon thereafter, they purchased their first Colorado home. Then they were off to Denver and Greeley where he finished college and was invited into professional Boy Scouting. His first assignment was Grand Junction, which drew them up the Crystal and Frying Pan with the Scouts and their own family camping trips.

Then the Thomson family was off to Concordia and Overland Park, Kansas,

Iowa and back to Colorado Springs. Luckily for all of us, before they ran out of new places to move to, they found and bought a twenty-four by twenty-eight shell of a house on Redstone Boulevard in 1971-'72.

The Thomson "bungalow" circa 1972. "We called it what it was-a shack!" Courtesy of the Thomson Collection

103

Thomson clan, circa early 1970s. Courtesy of the Thomson Collection

A CASTLE BY ANY OTHER NAME

First off, there was no plumbing and no wiring. It was one of the miners' cabins originally built in 1898, and one of four in a row. All four are inhabited today. If not for interior decorations, the line of sight is perfect aligned out the Thomson front window through all the other houses to the end house. Talk about precise construction. Well, except for this, that and the other.

"We were not so much fussy as we were 'economically challenged' so it took three years of hunting before we saw the 'For Sale' sign between this and the house next door," Shirley said. "Even though it needed more work, we decided we liked this one better." They called Doris Ferguson, the listing Realtor, and went to check it out.

"We had looked in Hermits Hideaway and up the Frying Pan," Shirley said. "Then we realized, as retirees, we needed to be 'on pavement' if we were going to live up here." Shortly after, they plunked down a payment. "We told the kids it was a bungalow. Between us, we called it what it was—a shack!"

Shirley showed me the 1971 Montgomery Ward electrical and plumbing books available back then and told me how, day after day, David pored over the pages. Finally, she told him, "Put the book down, it's time to go to work!" It can be said Shirley is short and sweet—in many ways. And, it was Shirley that pulled all the wires through the tiny crawlspace under the cabin.

SUMMERS MADE FOR MEMORIES

Summer vacations for son John and daughters Janet and JoAnn, their spouses and children, became the experience of a lifetime, helping build Mom and Dad's crowning achievement in the "Ruby of the Rockies" Redstone. It was the beginning of a thirty-year plus relationship with the Upper Crystal River Valley that wouldn't be nearly as nice without the Thomson tall and short couple.

In spite of the honeymoon "differences of opinion," David enjoyed a seventy-five, yes, seventy-five year career in the Boy Scouts. He was just as focused, dedicated and determined to keep the Marble Community Church afloat.

"PERSISTANCE"—DAVID'S LIFELONG MOTTO

Shirley believes that David's power of persistence came from his Grandfather, who invented more than one hundred different products that became necessary parts of life, such as electric meters, even when they were not "officially" recognized by the Department of Patents.

So it comes as no surprise that difficult projects were David's forte. Besides beginning the rehab and expansion of their "bungalow" in 1972, Shirley and David became pivotal members of the-then nearest community church which, at the time, was up in Marble. The Church at Redstone across the street did not exist. Back then, Sunday services were held during the summers only and visiting ministers were enticed with the congregation's pledge to "furnish a house (sometimes trailer) for a week for a sermon." Methinks there must have been a

David certainly felt rain drops before Shirley did but they shared plenty of sunny days in their six decades of marriage. Courtesy of the Thomson Collection

Shirley and David share one of a multitude of happy memories in their Redstone back yard. Courtesy of the Thomson Collection

rash of ministerial vacations in Marble. After all, remember, we're as close to Heaven as one can get without checking in. What minister wouldn't want that experience?

The Marble Community Church had belonged to the Episcopalian diocese in Denver. They allowed use of the church but would not give it to the community.

Some publications of Marble history such as Oscar McCollum's *Marble, A Town Built on Dreams, Volume 1* detail the evolution and (of course) politics surrounding the church structure from the time it was moved to Marble from Aspen in 1908.

Services were held in the heydays of Marble in the early 1900s until the early forties when the quarry finally shut down. Remember Kareen and Raquel Loudermilk of Heartbreak Hotel fame (Chapter 13)? The two teenage girls led song and prayer meetings in the old building during their summers here and these began to attract attention to the church in the fifties. By 1960, there was enough of a congregation to adopt the name of Marble Community Church. Reverend Dr. Frederick Udlock, a retired professor of religion at Hastings College in Hastings, Nebraska who lived outside Marble, became first a part-time, then full-time minister.

By the time David and Shirley arrived on the scene, the nearly hundred-year-old church was in a dangerous state of disrepair.

NO? GEE, SORRY. I CAN'T HEAR YOU.

David's motto became his mighty shield to deflect the nays of the diocese as he worked to have the building deeded to the church community. "Nos didn't

Grandpa David reading Christmas stories. Courtesy of the Thomson Collection

turn him off," said Shirley. After he did a thorough inspection of his own, he asked the diocese to do an engineering study of the building. The studies came back with a hundred sixty-seven things wrong with the place. The next conversation David had with them was when they called and said, "How would you like to have a church?" The church was incorporated in 1982 and the papers drawn up by retired judge Fred Malo.

After a period of summers and holidays only, the church started up year-round until the early nineties when the church went back to summer sermons only. In the late nineties, Pastor Linda Arocha of Aspen sang and preached to the small congregation on a part-time basis. Interest began to build again and the membership grew to the point that Pastor Arocha was asked to minister year-round, which she did until 2006. Today, Pastor Lafe Murray and his wife Lori are the church's interdenominational shepherds.

I asked Shirley why they would attend a church clear up in Marble, especially during heavy winters, when there's a nice, beautiful, big church directly across the street from the Thomson home.

"We have loyalty up our spine," she replied. She, as church treasurer since the seventies, and David as a powerfully motivating force, have witnessed "many miracles" as Shirley explained, with the tiny church over the years. They couldn't have possibly even considered for a moment to switch for convenience sake, what with all those miracles they've seen manifested.

RETIREMENT IS A LOT OF WORK!

David's leisure time was spent working on all kinds of projects, from his beloved Boy Scouts to shortwave radio, golf and fishing. "He professed to fish, but I never saw any," Shirley shrugged.

David substitute taught for the K-12 Roaring Fork School District for many years. David also kept active in Redstone and church activities. Shirley, by the same token, served on the Redstone Water and Sanitation District as secretary-treasurer for twelve years plus all the aforementioned associations, and even pulled a stint as Marble Town Clerk. "A very short stint," reminded Shirley.

Shirley and David's family tree branches out to three children, eight grand-children, eight great grandchildren and their extended family of an AFS student, Carlos Ceretti of Italy. In 2008, with Matriarch Shirley at eighty-five and the youngest girl—Kaelina Matthews—at sixteen months, four generations of the Thomson clan gathered for a huge family reunion. Their lives will forever be impacted by a charmed little bungalow in Redstone, Colorado, where, in a certain light, it positively glows golden with love.

The Thomson family reunion, Marble 2008. Shirley is fourth from the right in sunglasses. Courtesy of the Thomson Collection

Chapter 16

CHAIR MOUNTAIN STABLES

Since the first day the Utes acquired their horses from the Spaniards, riding horseback was, and arguably still is, the better mode of transportation to truly gain a high-mountain experience. Which is probably why horseback rides are so popular in this valley.

ON TOP OF THE WORLD

Chair Mountain Stables, behind the coke ovens on the west side of the highway in Redstone is one of, if not the longest running stables up here. Wrangler Chris Bernat, with his wife Kat and son Jeremiah operated Chair Mountain Stables from 1997 until 2004. He had worked there from 1992, and he and Kat were married there. Chris told me how he got to this area when he first came to Marble via Vermont, Wyoming and Crested Butte.

"I am originally from back East," Chris said. "One thing or another got me to Buffalo, Wyoming where I first learned wrangling on a dude ranch, then later on to Crested Butte. My former bosses of the Irwin Lodge, Gary and Patsy Wagner, had moved to Marble and taken over the remains of what was once the Mountain View Inn at the entrance of town." said Chris. He helped Gary and Patsy gut and rebuild the run-down building into a restaurant and room rentals and they named it the Crystal River Way Station.

Top, these crude log cabins were constructed by miners at Old Redstone, located on the west side of the Crystal River. Photo courtesy of "Crystal River Pictorial", Dell McCoy. Below, one of those cabins became the office of Chair Mountain Stables a hundred years later. Courtesy of Bernat collection

The Wagners also remodeled the main house, which became The Inn at Raspberry Ridge, Patsy's charming bed and breakfast operation since 1990. Chris explained how he, with friend and fellow former Irwin Lodge employee, Ron Hannah, flipped burgers and whatever else needed doing at the 'Way Station until it sold again. Chris heard about a wrangling job down in Redstone. In the spring of 1992, Chris met up with Tom and Claudette Mainer, originally from Huntsville—guess where?

IT'S THOSE TEXANS AGAIN!

I'm not making this up. It seems that Texans are in every story I dig up about this valley! They all must have good taste in vacation destinations.

Tom Mainer was a former banker who decided to make a lifestyle change when he moved his family to Redstone in 1987. Tom and Claudette named the stables in honor of the magnificent view of Chair Mountain, as well as their Chair Mountain Ranch and Cabins business a little ways up Highway 133, at the turnoff of County Road 3. Their stables were originally with the ranch but when the lease on the land behind the coke ovens in Redstone became available, they moved the horses to the more accessible location. Onsite were original coal worker cabins that had been turned into the then Redstone Stables.

Chris said that the Joe, Jerry and Jeff Burtard family first started horseback riding in Redstone in the sixties and seventies. They were living in the carriage house of the Redstone Castle and would originate rides on what is now the back parking lot of the Redstone Inn. At that time, the horses were stabled across the river.

Readers will remember Mike Schilling of the Crystal Valley Manor (Chapter 13). One of his many stories was his days as an operator and backcountry guide of the Redstone Stables during the seventies and eighties.

When the Redstone Stables sold and moved, the tack room of the old main cow camp behind the ovens became home-sweet-home for the Mainer family

Billy Greer hitches up Tom and Jerry, the famous white Percherons for a winter's sleigh ride to the Redstone Castle. The popular Chair Mountain Stables worked pretty much year round. Courtesy of Bernat collection

with their three sons and daughter. They gradually built up one of the most popular family horseback riding experiences in the area. "That's what they would tell me anyway," drawled Tom when we caught up with him by phone back in Huntsville.

"We built up the trails back in Coal Basin," he said, "which was spread over thousands of acres." The Mainers acquired the backcountry hunting permits from Kelly Lyons for Huntsman Ridge and Hayes Creek by that fall for their first hunting trips, and Tom later purchased the permits for Spring Creek and Coal Basin.

"We would open by Mother's Day and always try to be the first with horses ready for tourists coming upvalley," Chris said of those fourteen years under his well-worn glove. "At the highest, we would have thirty head of horses but, but we usually ran twenty to twenty-five head."

GITTIN' IN A GOOD GAIT

Chair Mountain Stables soon became known for its care with children during their first riding experiences. "Kids would come back year after year and say, 'Hey, that's Shotgun' or 'That's Penny.'" he said. "They'd remember riding that horse from when they were real little." Their meadows became a popular location for weddings and receptions. And every fall, Chris and his staff would head out to run hunting camps. "We had work pretty much year 'round except in early spring," said Chris, "because we also did sleigh rides with Tom and Jerry through Redstone and to the Castle during...."

111

Chris Bernat (left) with his wranglers. Women make the best wranglers, we learn. Far right is Roger who kept everyone in stitches with his misadventures. Courtesy of Bernat collection

Sh-h-h-sh! Amidst our summery frame of mind, we want not to mouth that *un*mentionable word here of a "certain" season. But, yes, sleigh rides were oh-so magical with a stunningly huge, pair of white Percherons named Tom and Jerry. Don't get me wrong; sleigh and carriage rides are still a wonderful experience today, but there was something quite extraordinary about those two draft horses. Gigantic yet graceful, gliding through quiet, still, starry nights in a perfectly matched gait, Tom and Jerry will be remembered by many.

Long-time wrangler and well-known local figure, Billy Greer, became Chris's good friend as they worked together for the Mainers. Business grew steadily over the years, by the best possible way—word of mouth. "It proves that it is always important to have the support of the community," reminded Chris, "and we worked hard to keep their trust and support." Never truer words spoken. We've seen businesses that work and those that don't. At least up here, support by the locals can make all the difference.

WE SEE BY YOUR OUTFIT...WHEN IS A HATTED, BOOTED COWBOY NOT? WHEN HE'S A "LITTLE MARY."

I learned a lot as Chris explained to this greenhorn the difference between cowboys and wranglers. "Cowboys take care of the cows, wranglers take care of the horses. And somewhere in there were the 'Little Marys,'" he said, grinning. Who were they? "Little Marys" are the beginners, no experience yet, so they got to do whatever they were called upon to do. "You didn't want to be a 'Little Mary' very long." said Chris.

Although there were a number of male wranglers that worked at Chair

Top, Tom and Claudette Mainer, below, Kat, Jeremiah and Chris Bernat. Courtesy of Bernat collection

Mountain Stables during the years, I was surprised to learn that women make up a majority of wranglers. "They are basically better with clients but we had both, by all means," he said.

One honest-to-goodness mountain man joined up with Chris in 1997-'98 as his right-hand helper. Ira Cossins is one who knows this backcountry in his sleep as well as the back of his hand and is familiar with all those of the natural world within. As expertly as he can skin an elk, Ira can wield the lightest feathery brush. His pen-and-ink drawings and oils are displayed in many a home and business. When we had a coffeebar our first winter in Marble, Ira held art classes there. We found him to be an incredibly effective instructor for beginners and intermediates alike. Everyone loved how much they learned in Ira's classes.

IF ONLY HE'D STOP LAUGHING

I asked Chris if he had any stories to share about his wranglers. Folks, here's what happened. Chris nodded his head yes, began to smile, then chuckle, then laugh, then cough and nearly choke from said laughter, meanwhile tears streamed down his reddened eyes and scrunched-up face.

We've all been there. You envision some scene where someone said or did the funniest thing you've ever seen and you re-live it all over again. All Chris could sputter was something about "our beloved Roger" and something about an "authentic" twenty-dollar Bowie knife Wrangler Roger had picked up at a pawn shop one payday.

"Roger was one of our best, favorite and most devoted but also, most unlikely wranglers," Chris said. "He looked just like [the comic character] Sad Sack with coke bottle-thick glasses he must have gotten from his granddad." Chris wheezed as he tried to catch a breath. He related some funnies about Roger breaking in a mule named Taco (or was it the other way around?), and one about a favorite pistol Roger owned where the cylinder—held in by a sixteen-penny nail—would fall out every time he shot the gun. He'd ask Chris, "What do you think I should do about it?" When told to throw it away so he would-n't get hurt, Roger took real offense against his "pride and joy."

I heard a smile forming over the phone when I asked Tom the same ques-tion. He agreed. "One day, I picked up a skinny, little guy hitch-hiking from Carbondale," Tom said. "He ended up working for me for over fifteen years. Roger always made us laugh." Roger moved to Huntsville to continue working for son Tommy Mainer at his outfitting business but we're told he has since moseyed on back to Colorado somewhere.

Since I can't get Chris to stop laughing, guess we'll have to only imagine the Roger-isms that can, years later, still bring tears to a grown man's eyes. You'll just have to ask Chris for a Roger story yourselves.

Chapter 17

MARBLE COMMUNITY CHURCH

Found out I'll never be an "OldTimer" even when I become an oldtimer up in Marble. I got that major difference straightened out at a coffee klatch with the last few of the legendary Marble OldTimers here for their twenty-first annual reunion on July 19, 2008. They are quite time-specific: Marble, circa 1930s. The Depression Days.

BOY, ARE YOU YOUNG!

As far as they are concerned, all the rest of us since then are still sucking our thumbs. And they made their point. How many of those who think of them-selves as being here "longerthan" sat behind a desk every day—K-12—in the very same school building here today? Or played an instrument in the school band? Or went to the Marble movie theater? Or...and here's the knockout punch...are proud to say that they lived here when everyone in Marble got along and helped each other out?

We scan the horizon. How many are out there? Well, get in line behind K-12 Marble grad, Esther Baumli Sanchez, and her classmates—sister Rose Baumli Razzano; the brothers Petrocco, John and Ercole; and sisters Mary Wood Coles and Dorothy Wood Orlosky. They certainly deserve our acknowledgement and respect as "THE Marble OldTimers."

Top, the Marble Community Church was first brought by railroad car from Aspen in 1908. Below, after the belfry was added. Courtesy of Marble Community Church

IT WASN'T DEPRESSING THEN

Even in the Depression days, they all agree that they never felt "lack." They told how the huge Italian and Swiss families here then were very self-sufficient by trading with their neighbors for the things they all needed. This is a different Marble than we hear about from more recent oldtimers from the fifties on. Marble was notorious for the fact that when only a few families lived here, no one got along in Marble. What happened? Did hard times make for more connected, caring neighbors?

By the way, those real oldtimers were quite a lively group of octogenarians, sharing stories and laughing as they would mention one name or another—"characters"—as Ercole Petrocco called them. They were all smiling, uncomplaining and proud of their ages, and totally positive about their beloved memories of their life in this remote mountain mining town.

This group has attended reunions most every year since the Wood sisters, Dorothy and Mary, organized the first event in 1987. They come from as far away as New York, New Orleans and California, as well as Colorado Springs and Grand Junction. The first year, there were more than one hundred fifty attended, In 2008, it was six. "It's our only trip of the year, and we love it when we come back and I can see 'my' mountain, Whitehouse," said Esther smiling.

BLOW OUT THE CANDLES - WHERE'S THE HOSE?

The Oldtimers Reunion was not the only Anniversary of the Aged in 2008. On July 6, congregants and visitors attended the one hundredth anniversary of the Marble Community Church in its present site, ending with the unveiling and dedi-

Gathering of the faithful at the Centennial services, July 2008. Author photo

cation of "The Angel of Love," a marble sculpture created by local sculptor Connie Hendrix.

The one-century celebration began with services by Lafe Murray, current pastor of the interdenominational church. Peter and Becky Bone, Lori and Lafe Murray, Jeanette Bier and David and Cathy White provided the music. Many memories of the Marble Community Church were shared during the services, which continued at a potluck supper in the Fellowship Hall.

Lafe read from letters sent to the church. One was from Pastor Bruce Gledhill. "We, at your sister congregation, the Church of Redstone, rejoice and praise God along with you for the Lord's wonderful provision for you. Our majestic God knows our needs long before we do, and by His divine power He sets things in motion to provide for us.

"You have been wonderful custodians, faithful stewards of this gift from God...we are one in spirit with you as you celebrate this milestone in the life of your church."

Another letter was from Reverend Sam Ritchey who was in a summer minister program at the Marble Church for eighteen years during the eighties and early nineties. He said, "Marble is one of the most spectacular places on earth." He described his first trip to the Crystal River Valley. "It was one of those 'Wow' experiences!" he wrote. He told of how he and his wife and children were provided housing for one week in exchange for their services on a Sunday morning. Reverend Sam conducted the service and his wife Nancy played the organ. His description of their housing as a home to "pack rats and other varmints," with a leaky black hose for their only water supply had the congregation in howls of laughter. Sam shared that he, Nancy and their children Amy and Eric, "felt more and more like locals over the years."

SUMMER OF LOVE? NOT FROM THIS RECTOR

George Drake spoke next. Once a seminary student from the United Church of Christ (yes, the same church as Obama and Reverend Wright in Chicago), he eventually became president of Grinnell College in Iowa and is now a retired history professor.

"Sue and I came up here as newlyweds forty-eight years ago," George said. "Back in 1960, the building existed, but was barely used. As the town became a ghost town in the mid-forties, the church became a ghost church. Services were revived in the late 1950s by the daughters of Wade and Wilma Loudermilk. They gave people the idea that somehow there would be enough summer population to merit some sort of ministry in the church.

"Nineteen sixty-one was an explosive summer for the church," George told the audience. "The Glenwood Springs newspaper featured one of our services. I soon got a call from the Episcopal priest in Glenwood Springs."

"I always thought it was better to ask permission to use someone's church." the rector said.

"'I always thought it was better to use the church than let it sit idle," replied George. "Besides, we have permission."

"Turns out we didn't," said George.

OOPS!

Stories and memoirs now record that the two well-intentioned teenage girls, Raquel and Kareen Loudermilk, who held their prayer meetings in the abandoned church, maybe "forgot" to ask permission from someone somewhere far away to use the church. Teens? Forgetting? How unusual. Yet, as Pastor Bruce's letter alluded, it turns out that they may have lit the match that sparked the firestorm that was needed to clear a path for the church and what it has become today.

Back to 1961: Suddenly, summer Sunday services had to come to a screeching halt. The rector came to lock them out the next weekend. Marble's faithful moved across the street, in the middle of a field, out in the open air. Probably in the rain too, you imagine?

THOSE NOSY REPORTERS!

"It happened that a Denver Post reporter was camping down at Bogan Flats," George said. "[He] saw us and wrote a story in the newspaper about a 'poor struggling group of worshippers' juxtaposed with photos of the totally available empty church building across the street with the sign in front that said St. Paul's Episcopalian Church.

Next thing you know, *Time Magazine* picked up the story about this little ousted church congregation in tiny Marble, Colorado. The then-religious world's spotlight turned this way. Today, it'd probably be getting a million hits on MySpace and FaceBook.

"Money from the Episcopalians came pouring into Marble," George continued, "most mortified by the publicity."

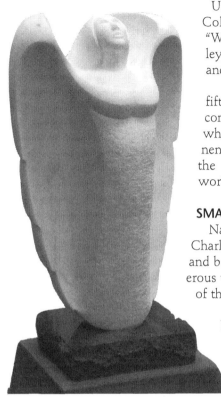

"Another of the vacation pastors was Skip Udlock, professor of religion of Hastings College in Nebraska," George added. "When Skip retired and moved to this valley, he became the first permanent pastor and thus began a real year-round church.

"That's the story I can tell of at least fifty of these one hundred years," George concluded. "It blows my mind to see what you folks have done—a) a permanent congregation, b) all the renovations, the construction, the parsonage, all the work you have done. Thank you."

SMALL BUT MIGHTY

Nancy Taylor told the congregation of Charles R. Jones, a summer service attendee and benefactor to the church. Charley's generous will provided for the land and building of the parsonage.

Shirley Thomson spoke of her husband David's persistence with the Episcopalian diocese in Denver after the publicity blitz until the day they called him and asked, "Do you want a church?"

Shirley also acknowledged the work and efforts of former resident Katie Updike. "The church was in serious disrepair," Shirley said. "Katie and the board found

The Angel of Love, Yule marble sculpture by Connie Hendrix donated to the Marble Community Church for its 100th birthday. Author photo

grants and ways to raise the matching funds to make the repairs we needed."

"We are small but mighty," Shirley emphasized with a punch—to great applause.

Reverend Linda Arocha-Boylan shared memories during her tenure as shepherd of this mountain flock between 1997 and 2005. Some were about former Marble mayor Wayne Brown and his dog Corkie who would come up to the altar and take communion. Eventually, between the aging congregation and the aging Corkie, tripping over one another became a real hazard. Corkie was banned from the church—the end of yet another unique era.

Linda's husband, Bob Boylan strolled everyone down his dozen-year memory lane and had everyone laughing at his description of deep winter services when everyone wore their warmest coats because the noisy old furnace had to be shut off in order to hear Linda's sermon. He spoke of summer residents, Lu and Doyle Duke. "They were always dressed up, making the rest of us looked like clods," Bob said. "They sat right up in the front row." Bob related how upon a visit to the Dukes's home in Graham, Texas, he and Linda stayed in a bedroom that had recently been renovated by Doyle, including all the electrical work. "We thought we needed a bedroom on the first floor for when we get older." Doyle told them, who was then ninety.

By the time Bob recounted all the fundraising potlucks and other church-related events that he remembered, he asked that all who had participated in any one or more of those activities to please stand. No one was sitting down.

Brad and Laurel Larson were in the audience. They had married in the church. Along with the congregation's, they were celebrating their twelfth anniversary. Brad told how they thought it was a great deal when Wayne Brown told them the use of the church for their wedding would cost them $75. "When we asked how much more for the weekend," said Brad, "Wayne said that WAS for the entire weekend!"

ANGEL OF LOVE EMBRACES ONE AND ALL

The centennial celebration continued outside as everyone gathered in a circle on the lawn next to the church for the unveiling and dedication of a gift from local sculptor, Connie Hendrix, the *Angel of Love*.

"It has been quite a process," explained Connie. "My grandfather once said, 'Do something you love and you will be a success.' Art has been good to me and I want to honor Clyde and Lola Wright."

Connie then described the details to get to this day's dedication. Connie's sculpture weighs about four hundred pounds. Marble blacksmith Dan Prazen made a steel pedestal and a friend, Roger Seal, who passed away, made the black granite part of the pedestal. The white marble with gold veining in the piece is from the Colorado Yule Marble Quarry from Treasure Mountain in Marble, "the primo marble that you can get out of the quarry," Connie said of her Angel of Love.

This angel speaks to all as they pass by on the road. She is the perfect gift for a one-hundred year celebration of the Marble Community Church.

Chapter 18

COLORADO'S LITTLEST CHARTER SCHOOL
IN THE HEART OF MARBLE

Do our dear local readers happen to notice that low, soughing sound coming up through the valley the latter part of every August? Inspector ClueCharr here traced the phenomena to a collective, massive sigh of relief from dazed parents. It happens when the kids are back in school. The kids are happy. The teachers are happy. No doubt, parents are the happiest.

HOWEVER....
Adapting quickly to ageing rationale, I've decided that "old," "history" and "new" and "reincarnation" are all relative words. I'm reminded of such when I look at the photo of the historic Marble High School building so beloved by our Marble oldtimers with whom we visited last chapter. Fast-forward some seventy years. Same building, same blackboard, same small classrooms, and same bunch of happy faces behind their desks; lots of "sames" we see, but an entirely different historic school today.

Installation of the temporary modular classroom while the historic school building (far right) is repaired. The school is reopened after nearly fifty years with the organization of local parents for a charter school. Courtesy of Marble Charter School

SHHH! QUIET! LET'S LOITER IN THE HALL

The double doors of Marble High School were locked for the last time in 1948. There aren't but a few folks today that remember that significant event.

It's hard to imagine what "success" looked like in the beautiful valley surrounding the booming town of Marble that justified the marble quarry's successful mining endeavors in the early nineteen hundreds. As mining towns went, it sure wasn't that pretty. It suffered the indignities of massive denudation. Often mentioned by the oldtimers today is that they can't find or don't recognize certain areas in town because of all the regrowth.

Early photographs attest to how most trees surrounding the town's settlement were cut down for structure of commercial buildings, houses, workers' cabins and their outhouses. Mining structures dotted the hillsides around the marble quarry operations. Abandonment was next. The town declined further after the quarry's difficulties, financial and logistical, in getting the marble shipped out of the valley. Accidents and deaths were but part of the price paid. The quarry finally shut down and most workers and their families moved downvalley. The floods (Mother Earth's tears?) of the early forties collapsed most of the remainder of the town. There was no more community in Marble; ergo, there was no more school. The land and school building lay dormant for nigh some thirty winters—the school bells quieted, the building taking leave of its lumbered supports.

By the early-mid sixties, there were but a couple households with children. The Upper Crystal Valley was largely abandoned, and only sparsely inhabited by hippie-types, hermits and other assorted mountain characters, say locals from the day.

We pick up that soughing sound again—there's a change in the air blowing through the deteriorating school building—or is it emanating from the old school's outdoor two-holer? The school's transformation came about after the Marble church's reincarnation. Coincidence, you say? Indeed. That word, prefaced by "whadda," is oft on many lips in Crystal Valley stories told.

LOITERING, PAST AND PRESENT, LEADS TO THE SAME CLASSROOM CORNER

Teeny, tiny Marble garnered national attention in *Time Magazine* when the two young Loudermilk girls started up prayer services in an abandoned church

A real pied piper leads the schoolchildren to their interim classrooms at the Crystal River 'Way Station. Courtesy of Marble Charter School

building in their slumbering town. After a few summer services outdoors, the ousted congregation moved to the deserted school building for a short time in the early seventies, with pews donated by the Aspen Music Festival. Marble-ites can be quick at recycling pretty much anything.

It wasn't until the marble quarry reopened in the early 1990s, with housing cheaper than in the Roaring Fork Valley, that young families found the remote, alternative lifestyle in the backcountry appealing again. Soon, Marble had young lifeblood coursing through the overgrown streets and rotting buildings of the old-time days.

We heard octogenarians Esther Sanchez and Erocole Petrocco reminisce as students "back when;" they ice skated along Third Street and snow shoed their way to and from school. Today's students ice skate at the Millsite Park along Third Street and snow shoe their way to and from school. What's changed?

WELL, SINCE YOU ASKED...

The Marble Charter School is the smallest in the Colorado Charter School network. It's one of the first twenty-five charter designations in Colorado made in the early nineties. And, in the course of its reincarnation as a full-time school again, Marble and its National Historic school building garnered even more face time with major media newspaper and television.

The current-day school's teeter-totter existence in the old Marble High School building has not been without challenges of every imaginable sort.

Physically, the century-old wood structure was crumbing from without and within on its solid base of dazzlingly white marble. The Gunnison Watershed School District (GWSD) was probably only too happy to agree to donate the building to the newly-formed Marble Historical Society (MHS) for one dollar plus the cost of title transfer. A "work-in-progress report" from parent Katie Updike said the following: "MHS submitted the building to the National Historic Register of Buildings and began a museum. The one caveat in the title transfer was that the school district (per policy) included a deed restriction that limited the use of the property for a community use. If the property ceased to serve the public, the property would revert to the school district. The organizers of the MHS took their mission seriously and stabilized the deteriorating condition of the building, primarily with a new roof and by boarding or screening windows."

Marble Charter School, Grand Opening, September 22, 1995. A great day for the children who no longer had to endure 2-3 hour round-trips to Carbondale for school. Courtesy of Marble Charter School

This writer remembers early conversations with Wayne Brown, former president of MHS, occasional mayor of Marble and happy raconteur who loved to share his stories of the history of Marble with students, visitors and residents. It was Wayne who told me of the charter idea that he said some "city folk" talked about for a couple years. He spoke of the Colorado Charter School Law that permits communities to establish their own public schools. There was— *coincidentally*—a sub-section for a Rural Charter School Network, of which Marble was one of five schools. In these remote areas, the schools were a recognized social and community linchpin and qualified for certain grants.

Wayne looked me in the eye and said, "Our [MHS] board told them (the parents) that they had to get their work done first. If they could get the charter designation and the grant monies to fix the building, of course, the historical society would want them to use the building." Wayne was an ardent supporter of the school and loved entertaining each year's upper grade class with his famous slide show presentation of the history of Marble.

In the summer of 1994, Katie Updike drafted a charter school application while still living in Chicago. "GWSD Superintendent Mike Richardson made it clear that he would support the charter application," she said, "but only if the parent organizers could demonstrate that the school would be able to meet academic standards."

CHALLENGES EVERYWHERE—PICK ONE

Katie was one of a number of part-time residents and Ph.D.s who lent their collective brains for the grant writing and fundraising needed to start a remote community public school. With enthusiastic support by almost all of the parents who wanted to end the grueling two to three hour round-trips their children had to take to Carbondale, they organized themselves and held a town meeting in April of 1995 to inform the community about the intended formation of the school and the use of the building.

The upshot of Katie's report: "Most community members were intrigued with the idea of keeping the younger children off the long bus rides, although there were a handful of residents who were concerned that the renovation of the school building would destroy its character. In the end, the plans moved forward on behalf of the school."

Coincidentally (again), part-time resident Tommy Thompson happened to own a company that leased modular buildings for schools and bank branches down in Arizona. He negotiated a lease favorable to the school. The unusually kind terms meant that the school could rescind the lease and eliminate the unnecessary expense of the modular (and the crowded addition to the MHS property) as soon as possible to renovate and occupy the main building."

Not to gloss over the trials and tribulations of the school's renovations, and the discovery therein of even more critical repairs needed; but, inevitably the first day of school happens. Uh-oh. This particular year's school bell wasn't quite ready to ring. The modular classroom was "it" and "it" was still in Arizona. Without today's ability to GPS monitor progress, it took a while for the children awaiting their magical mystery school to find out that "it" was having a dramatic journey along the way.

Blending old with new desks, the first class is ready to begin. Courtesy of Marble Charter School

DON'T SHOOT THE MESSEN... ER, DRIVER

One of the trucks hauling the two halves of the trailer ran into a bridge. Not fatal but the building would need repair. The Colorado border was still a long ways off. Then one truck lost an axle...not one, but two. The modular company sent its manager out to the two trucks. Soon there was a three-way telephone relay between the company, the manager and Katie's office in Marble.

Scrambling for classroom space, the school temporarily convened in the Crystal River Way Station (the old Mountain View Inn) at the entrance to Marble. The restaurant and home was owned by Bob and Miriam Leone who stepped up to the dire need. Of course, there was enthusiastic fanfare and publicity to record the historic moment that only a handful of Marble students could generate. Newspapers and television crews filmed Opening Day, with all the students assembled in front of the old building. The vintage school bell was symbolically rung and a real pied piper, flute in hand, led the first twenty-six students down the road to the Way Station for classes. That night, Channel 9 NBC News in Denver used the Marble footage for its "Back to School" centerpiece.

Meanwhile, back on the Interstate, the two mastadonian trucks were finally in Colorado and lumbering their way between Grand Junction and Glenwood Springs. One of the drivers looked at the mountains ahead. His flatlander feet refused to move further. The company management "hit the ceiling," and Katie got a call to see if anyone was available with a commercial driver's license who could take over the last two hours of driving. Katie called Marble's mayor at the time, Joe Manz. He was up for the challenge until he met the allegedly intoxicated driver who had an unyielding control of the steering wheel. Words were exchanged. Knowing Joe, ahem, *of course* they were words of calm, comfort and reassurance. Ha!

Next scene: Mayor Joe commandeered the lead truck, carrying one half of the Marble classroom over the Grand Avenue Bridge in Glenwood Springs and through almost every red light on Grand Avenue. The second driver followed, with local resident Robert Wagner bringing up the rear, with hazard lights flashing. The hangdog driver, his head hung out the passenger window, was only too glad his personal nightmare was about over.

WE'RE SO EXCITED—LET'S EAT!

Back in Marble, the community was abuzz with anticipation. Neighbors arranged an impromptu potluck lunch for the eager families at the county shop while Gary Bascom, a volunteer firefighter and parent, brought out the fire truck with sirens blaring to lead the buildings into town and to the school. Everyone in the community lined the road into town, hooting and cheering the successful arrival of their new schoolroom. Not a bit of insulation in the southern-made modular, they found out later, but it did have an indoor toilet. Life was good at Marble's new school.

FIRST SCHOOLTEACHER—COOL APLOMB, NO ALARM HERE

The first teacher to begin classes in the revived Marble school system was Katharine Emsden, who moved back to her home state from teaching in Massachusetts into the "big kids" (fourth through eighth grade) classroom.

"As for my academic program, it's many a teacher's dream to create their own," said Katharine from her home in La Veta, Colorado. "I remember my successor, Steve Finn, being duly impressed with what I had set in place. Mornings were structured reading, math, language arts with group books, work books and individualized assignments, and goals I made weekly for each child. Afternoons were thematic and multi-age, covering history, geography and science with daily writing. One winter hike became a contest to find three different species of insects in the snow."

Katharine said how she came to no longer be surprised at Monday morning's Show and Tell. "One time one of the girls told of an accident with serious injury to her dad when a dead elk on a runaway sled ran over him," she said. "Another time, a young boy came to school with a bloody rock where his dad had shot a bear." Dissecting owl pellets to identify their last meals may not be on your kid's school curriculum, but it was a routine part of school for these youngsters. The MCS students were hardy souls who made the best of their primitive school facility. Katharine said, "MCS organized a snow sports day for neighboring schools. We did well in all events, maybe because we often snow-shoed right off the front porch, following the river to Beaver Lake."

Wayne Brown and Katharine arranged for some of the old desks to be used in her upper-grades classroom. Because she had done brass rubbings, she had the children do rubbings of their desk tops, including all the graffiti of students from 1912 to 1948. "I told them there better not be any additional markings at the end of the school year."

RESPECT YOUR ELDERS AND YOUR HISTORY—
MARBLE STUDENTS MIRROR ONE ANOTHER

The students eventually got into the school building, converting the old coal-bin room into the lower-grades classroom, with the main floor classroom for the fourth through eighth grades. They were just as enthusiastic and excited as their predecessor students, Esther and Ercole, to daydream at their desks and look out the class windows to *their* mountain, Whitehouse.

The adjacent main floor room and the upper floor rooms were reserved for the museum that early MHS docents helped reinstall after the renovations. During the early days of the charter school, the students became junior docents during the school year and were able to learn and connect even more with their surroundings as they gave tours to eager tourists.

REPORT CARD TIME

There were many occasions to celebrate in the successes of the school's early growing years. Not just effusive parental pride, it was evident with cold, hard

Artist rendering by Marble resident, Charlie Manus, of the new Marble Charter School and Crystal Valley Preschool building, which is under construction at press time. Courtesy of Marble Charter School

facts. In spite of the incredibly limited facility and supplies, the achievement levels of the children rose every year. More than once, Marble Charter School had the best record in the state. Statistics in a small school can be startling, Katie's report noted. Today, as the school bursts at the building's seams, endeavors are being made with the support of GWSD to bring additional classrooms and educational tools up to the twenty-first century.

As Katharine shared stories of her students then and now with those whom she has still has contact, she has good memories of Marble Charter School. "Those were two very special years for me," she said.

In spite of all adversities—physical, political, spatial, logistical, not to mention the bitterly cold winters in the modular—the teachers, community volunteers and growing student population have turned this into the best little public charter school in Colorado.

The local elections of 2008 included a bond issue for Gunnison County schools. Marble received a substantial award to expand the school facilities with an additional building that will include classrooms, a kitchen and community room. Yea! The groundbreaking begins!

Chapter 19

HUNTING IN THE HIGH COUNTRY

Back in the Utes' day, the traditional roles of hunters and gatherers provided food for the family. Today, it's called, "Who's going to the grocery store?" But many in the Crystal Valley still basically do the same as the earliest residents for our food. Locate. Cull. Cultivate. Clean. Preserve. And come wintertime, burrow in or get out. Sounds pretty progressive, huh?

AS GATHERERS GATHER, SO DO HUNTERS HUNT

Had this writer the opportunity, I'd don camouflage—if I could find it—or put on a bright orange vest and go forth into the hinterlands to get first-hand this chapter's stories. I figure the only way to learn what it's like to go high-altitude hunting is to...Whoa! Hold on to your long johns.

And dear readers, you thought I was going to say, "I'm really going hunting." NOT quite! But I did the next best thing: I rubbed antlers with some local hunters, past and present. In huff'an'puff detail, as one hunter described, I learned what it is like to wake up in the frozen dark of very early morn, dress like the Pillsbury doughboy and tromp all over "here and gone" to crouch statute-still behind trees—totally silent, no less—for maybe twelve hours. That alone right there precludes Moi and her Chatty Cathy girlfriends. But the fun doesn't stop there. I learned to track the hunted by sticking a finger in yellow snow,

(areyoukiddingme?!), not to mention, sleep in frozen bedding in order to be stiff and cold all day…all in the name of "fun" and *really* high-dollar grocery shopping.

WHAT'S SO BAD ABOUT THE SUPERMARKET?

Given that the movie "Bambi" was this writer's first exposure to Elmer Fudd's Facts of Life, on its face, hunting seems cruel and unusual punishment all the way around. I grew up a city kid. Crying for days (still do) after the heartbreaking scene of orphaned Bambi frantically running to and fro, this girl-child thought, unless supermarkets shut down anytime during the rest of my lifetime, I'd have to skip the meat and live on beans and potatoes. That lasted until the next hamburger.

Living now in the middle of high altitude hunting country, I figured it was time to learn more about a typical hunting season up the Crystal. Perchance I could reprogram my biased opinions or perceptions. You know, "see the other side." *Gulp.* I try not to think about those two gorgeous bucks that, all summer, took to napping in the shade of a goose-neck trailer parked down our road. *Knot-hard swallow.* Can I tie them up behind the shed and protect them? At least I haven't named them.

Come hunting season, the orangies look like a waltzing pumpkin patch on these hillsides. All the service providers—bed, food, camp suppliers—are slammed. I found a fifties-era ad for the Redstone Inn. Many an out-of-state hunter opted for the nightly hot showers and plush beds. There are a number of quality outfitter businesses too. But there is a cadre of individual local hunters up here who hunt "the old fashioned way" (by themselves) and to those I turn to get a firsthand look at, uh, harvest time. Time to cull those herds and fill the freezers full of loin, sausage and chops. Not to mention share a pretty wild tale or two!

THE HUNTER AND GAME WARDEN STORY

Remember our story about Swiss Village Resort and the Wallace Parker family (Chapter 7)? Wallace had told us back then how his father was quite the hunter and fisherman from…guess where?…and how he naturally became a guide for family and friends that came out every year from same big boot state. When I visited again with Wallace and Naomi, he told me that these days he is "more successful in the backend of City Market."

He shared one story, swore it was true, names omitted to protect the less innocent. It's an "early days" hunting story from over in the Basalt area.

Seems a long-time farmer had taken his wagon out to get some firewood and to get a deer for the dinner table. Seems reasonable enough except it wasn't "officially" hunting season. The farmer got the needed deer right off the bat, laid it on the bottom of his wagon and proceeded to fill the wagon with wood. As he headed up the road towards home, he met up with the friendly game warden.

"Hey there, what'cha you been doing?"

"Oh, getting a little firewood."

They visited awhile longer until the warden told the farmer, "Better get on home now before your firewood bleeds to death."

Wallace prefers the relative leisure of fishing these days. As for hunting, he said, "You remember how. It is hard work to do it right. Unfortunately, hunters today violate the law and violate the ethics."

Wallace's wife Naomi then discussed the similar merits of high-mountain gardening for the relative rewards: two or three snow peas, a couple tiny tomatoes and a handful of okra. "For all the work you do, it's best to have a greenhouse up here," she said wisely. We three agree that getting food by gardening and hunting alone is as hard as it ever was.

Of course, as local gardeners reconcile and reseed, local hunters know that repetition breeds the same familiarity. With knowledge of one's surroundings and habits of the wildlife herein, they learn all the game trails, watering holes, bedding down sites. Even so, they are not always successful. Which reminds me of more coincidences and stories I've heard.

ANOTHER FAMILY OF NATIVES—FIVE GENERATIONS DEEP

One of my neighbors, Cole Wilson, is a fifth generation native in this valley. He hunts every year, having made his first kill at age six or seven. Cole was born and raised in Glenwood Springs. His maternal Great Great Grandfather Purdy came from Pennsylvania over [what

Young Master Bobbie Budlong, son of Judge C.E. Budlong just after slaughtering a 350 pound brown bear with his high power air rifle. Courtesy of "Scenes in and about Marble, Colorado." Circa 1910.

was eventually named] Purdy Mesa in Rio Blanco County, near Grand Junction. His father's family settled in Denver and his dad hunted in this area since the late sixties.

Cole's mother's side of the family settled in Glenwood Springs. Barb Embry said that her side of the family was more "nature lovers. "My dad wouldn't kill anything," she said. Barb still lives in Glenwood Springs. She remembered hearing stories about covered wagon trips; first Grandfather alone, later Grandmother with the children. She remembered stories of how they met and became friendly with the local Indians.

Barb talked about the young native boy Cole, who preferred to go out alone; in the snow, create an overnight lean-to and hunt squirrels. "I would find the skins in his closet," she said. "He would roast and eat them. He always seemed to have the know-how to live as a survivalist."

While hunter education is required for licensure today, to learn how to hunt at the side of one's dad is, no doubt, special. To hunt together over lifetimes is beyond measure. To hunt with a weapon made by one's dad is pretty special too. Turns out Cole's father, Ken, made all his own firearms and Cole still hunts today with the .58 caliber muzzleloader made by Dad.

We can safely assume this father-son lifeway today is a familiar repetition of five and more generations ago.

DON'T TRY THIS IN YOUR NECK OF THE WOODS

I asked Cole of any hunting experience that stood out the most in his mind.

"When I was fifteen years old," he said, "I worked for an outfitter who had me hide behind an old beaver dam. That was back when baiting bears was allowed...."

Excuse me? BAIT? Who? You?

Cole said how restaurants used to save food scraps that he and others would put in burlap bags to hang in trees to attract the bruin.

"The client had shot at the bear, wounding him," he said. "I looked up over the dam to see this big black bear running right at me." Luckily, certainly for our vegetarian readers, the bear ran on past Cole. "We tracked him until dark. Then we had to bring the dogs out the next day to find him."

WHEN YOU COULD STILL LIVE OFF THE LAND...
UH, THAT WOULD BE TODAY

Last, but not least by any measure, I visited with full-time Marble resident and avid hunter Robert Pettijohn.

"I got my first elk up here in '75," he said. "The hunting got me up here from Fruita. It was so green, we just stayed here." Robert said that he and his mother were born in the same Denver hospital but that they always lived out in the country. "I have relatives from Creede, Delta and on down," Robert said.

"I come from a whole family of hunting.We grew up on beans, potatoes, whatever in the garden. We ate elk hearts," he said. "Yes, it was a cheaper way

Robert Pettijohn has seen every side of hunting his thirty-plus years in Marble. He prefers to hunt solo. Author photo

of life. During the Depression, people up here got by. Peaches, apple orchards, farmers nearby, plus all the wildlife. Did you know you could make bread flour from cattails?"

Has the hunting here always been good?

"Mostly. Ever since I've been living here, there used to be a huge herd of elk over on the north side of Redstone, well over two hundred head in the seventies," he said. "Now there's maybe forty to fifty." Gosh, and here we ooh and ahh when we drive by today and see what's left of that "big" herd grazing over in Filoha Meadows. Perception sure is relative.

He said that in the Osgood days at the turn of the twentieth century, the government gave the miners in Redstone four elk—every day. Employees went out each morning to hunt and feed all the miners who worked in the coal mines. No licenses required back then. We think about how many years they did that, year-round. Seems though that they shot up all the big bulls, only the little ones were left. The herds naturally got smaller.

"The dark-colored herd elk we don't have anymore. I don't think they [Osgood's hunters] had any thoughts about the effects of their actions to future hunters…which is now," mused Robert. So, what happens next?

RESPECT. EDUCATION. RESPECT. EDUCATION. WHAT'S THIS GUY SAYING?

If a bit shy in front of a camera, Robert wasn't the least bit shy about his philosophy of hunting today.

"Respect is important," he said. "Give the animal you hunt respect. Respect your weapon. By the way, it's not a 'gun.' It's a 'firearm' or a 'weapon.' Learn the right way to use it. Learn respect for other guys out in the woods. Respect distances. This is not a firing range. Know what's behind your prey and what happens to a bullet shot through an elk at 150 yards."

Not surprising, alcohol is a problem in some places. Robert believes that the ones who are hunters don't drink when hunting. But the fact is others really come to socialize, spend campfire time with friends and relations and see who can bag the biggest bull…story.

"For the ones who drink all night; come morning, they go a few feet out in the woods and sit down," he said. "The animals are safe."

That's a good thing, right?

ONE'S BUCK FEVER IS ANOTHER'S BAMBI BAD DREAMS

Robert then told a story of one hunting accident, and another, and another.

"One guy was climbing out of a ditch up to the road," he said. "He grabbed a bush to pull himself up, another guy thought it was antlers and shot him in the shoulder.

"Another man was tracking an antelope with a scope," he continued."He shot and killed his son-in-law in the chest because the son-in-law was up close range. The shooter was too excited to realize where the weapon was pointed."

Some, said Robert, still don't respect the animals. He told how he and others witnessed an out-of-state father and son, both with cow elk tags, and how, as soon as they got up here, they saw animals come out of the pond. They shot immediately. It was a mother…and her calf right behind her. *Bambiiiiiii!* The game warden was called. Not a pleasant experience for anyone.

Needless to ask, Robert pretty much hunts alone. He continued with his view of the ugly side of hunting. "They come up, spend a lot of money," he said. "Some just shoot into the herd. They don't wait for a shot. It's ego. Some guys put their head down and just go. Meanwhile, all the animals have heard them and are long gone. I believe in 'Stop. Look. Listen.' This way you get to see nature. You get more efficient at it. The better the shot, the better the meat."

Robert said that during the past thirty years, a lot of hunters that he's seen need to get more educated…not just come out to kill. Do it right, he said. But as he and Wallace Parker and Cole Wilson all agree: To do it right is a lot of hard work. "If there is going to be any future to hunting, it's going to have to be more selective," said Robert.

A HAIR-RAISING EXPERIENCE

Any unusual incidents when out hunting? Robert cocked a eye over at me as he rubbed his left knee.

"Aw, well," he drawled, "it was some ten, twelve years ago. I was out hunting with a friend."

"One of the lucky times he hunted with someone else," interjected Robert's wife, Judy.

"We were up around Milton Creek," he continued. "It was early December, nearly the end of hunting season, twelve degrees out there. There was a lot of snow. Some thirty inches had fallen overnight."

Robert had just gotten a big elk when he slid on some stones, started an avalanche, and fell fifty feet down the steep mountainside. One of the big rocks blew out his knee. He asked if I knew the term "leg-shot" deer. I claimed ignorance, not sure I wanted to know.

"It's when a deer is wounded and keeps running with the shot leg dangling and bouncing around," he said. That was the way his friend described Robert's injury to him. "He could have gone a long time and not told me that."

"I laid out there for an hour or two before I could get up and move," with the help of his friend, he said. If that was an understatement, t'was nothing compared to the physician's diagnosis. When he finally got downvalley to see a doctor, Robert turned as white as the doc's coat when the doctor turned his knee all the way around. "Yep, it's broken."

For six weeks, Robert couldn't move at all. Judy said, "We had no insurance. The doctor told us we'd either need thirty thousand dollars for an operation or he'd have to take three months off work."

Happily, Robert is back to work and back to hunting. In fact, as we visited, he was preparing for a hunt on the morrow.

Chapter 20

THE THOMPSONS—ONE FAMILY'S
125 YEARS IN CARBONDALE HISTORY

2008. Last quarter. This period in history will be remembered as a time when it was incomprehensible to understand "trillions" of dollars of debt, "billions" in bank and stock losses, "millions" of homes and jobs losses…some say for the first time since the 1930s, or "Depression Days"…hence, a cloak of somber grey and brown melancholy weighs heavy on this writer these days.

HAS THIS HAPPENED HERE BEFORE?

Ah, yes. I remember now why it is important to preserve history. So we have the wherewithal to look back over our collective shoulders, see what we can learn about how people survived in times of great challenges and change. As for this valley's changes, I decided to go straight up to the horse's saddle, so's to speak, and talk to Lew Ron Thompson, a long-time local rancher.

"We have six generations that have lived in the Crystal Valley area," said tall, lanky Lew Ron, as I introduced myself at his home in Carbondale. Mount Sopris filled the southern-view window of a cozy home deftly built, melding past and present materials. Perhaps it's an insight as to how this one family has survived the changes in this valley through lo these many generations.

The Crystal Valley from the view of "Mr. Eagle", Rob Hunker, ColoradoAerialViews.com. Lower portion is north and includes the River Valley Ranch development. The Crystal River runs diagonal top to bottom.

The Thompson family was one of the first settlers here before 1876. Great grandfather, Myron came from Missouri for prospecting and mining. His wife passed on in St. Joe, and Myron went back and forth until he finally moved their children out. Colorado was still a territory then. His family was one of the first to become residents of the new Centennial State when Colorado became part of the Union that year, 1876.

PIONEERS PUT DOWN ROOTS

I asked about the Ute connection. "Oh, yes, the Utes weren't run out until the late 1880s," Lew Ron said. "Apparently, they got along with Myron because they didn't kill him."

His grandmother's side of the family came from Indiana to Gothic, Colorado (on

Lewis and Julia Thompson, left, with 3 of their 4 children and other family circa 1939. Courtesy of Thompson collection

the Crested Butte side) and from there over into the Crystal Valley. They too were into mining and "transportation." Lew Ron said that they provided the famous jack trains that were the only way to transport anything across the Rockies from Crested Butte to Aspen to the Front Range. They had more than five hundred donkeys that carried ore, goods and supplies back and forth from mining camps.

At some point, they decided mineral wealth wasn't so easy after all. Myron and family settled into farming and ranching basically because of the need for fodder and hay for his donkeys. One of Myron's eight children, Lew Ron's Great-uncle Alex, settled on a ranch next door to Dad Myron, now called Sustainable Settings (see Chapter Six). Eventually, between both sides of Lew Ron's families, they owned at one time something near three thousand flatland acres around and in present-day Carbondale, plus land up near Marble.

THAT'S CALLED "STAYING CLOSE TO HOME"

In this home where we visited, Lew Ron was born in 1942. "It wasn't at this location then," he said. "It was over on the other side of the river where River Valley Ranch is now. We moved it here in 2001."

Some of the home's hand-hewn logs came from a summer family cabin that sat on some two hundred acres in front of Melton Falls, near Marble. "Melton is my grandmother's maiden name," Lew Ron said. The present-day, and apparently incorrectly spelled, "Milton" Falls, can still be seen from County Road 3, across the Marble Memorial Airport.

"That cabin was empty during the winters," he said. "The family used it in the summer when they ran sheep up there. During Prohibition, it was broken into by some bootleggers. Their stills caught on fire and burned up the cabin. We didn't know it until spring when we'd come back upvalley. You could still see parts of their stills among the remains."

He told how some of the logs seen in his house now were numbered, transported down and incorporated into the home. "It is going to be moved one more time a couple hundred feet south," Lew Ron said. "The family has sold off the remaining acres but for my two and a third that we have. We'll have professional movers come and do it."

Don't let anyone tell you different. Lew Ron is a real "home-base" man!

Carbondale, circa 1902. Some three thousand acres of all the flat land in this photo belonged to the Thompson families at one point in time. The Ranch was most of the middle right, along the the hills on the right side. Courtesy of the Thompson collection

WHAT'S IN STORE? DON'T SAY, "QUE SERA, SERA."

Since I must have listened to too much radio on the way downvalley and dragged my morose mood into the discussion, I asked about how the Thompsons remember the Depression Days here.

"Our stories from Dad were that the Depression was a tough period of time for people who lost their money," Lew Ron said. "But this area probably survived fairly well considering it was a localized economy then, and they didn't need a whole lot from the outside."

THOUGHT THE DEPRESSION WAS TOUGH?

Lew Ron said that perhaps more devastating to this area than the Depression was when the Sherman Silver Act was repealed. Aspen had become one of the largest silver mining districts in the country. When silver was demonetized, its value fell through the floor, taking fortunes hard made with it. Not only for the newly un-wealthy, but even more so, the worker folk were hit hard. Suddenly, their livelihood was no more.

"Aspen went dead," Lew Ron said. "Some called it the 'quiet years,' it was more like the 'desperate years.' People couldn't get out, they had no jobs, no money nor

Lew Ron and Jackie Thompson (seated, right) and their family, representing six generations living in the Crystal River Valley. Courtesy of the Thompson collection

anywhere to go."

He told how his mom, Julia, was one of nineteen kids. They couldn't afford to feed all of them and so Julia, at age seven, was sent off to Grand Junction to live with an older sister at the time.

Gradually, the desperate years morphed into the aforementioned quiet years, when farming and cattle raising took place in the area. Land all around Aspen, Basalt and Carbondale became big family ranches where folks could provide for themselves and their surrounding communities.

Then in the late forties, the town of Aspen started coming back with the ski resort boom. Suddenly snow drove the markets more than silver. Skiing revitalized the economy and kept growing. And growing. And growing. And growing still. Pretty soon the development of resorts, businesses and housing—all part of becoming a town again—has encroached more and more onto all that wide open space not being used by, uh, *them*.

Wait. Stop. Haven't we seen this movie before? Isn't that what was said when the Ute Indians were forced out of this valley? *They* aren't using all this land. There are valuable resources here *we* can use." Who's *we*? Who's *them*?

How did it fare the second time around—people being forced out of not only their land, but an inherited way of life held sacred for a long time?

SAD STATE OF AFFAIRS

"In a way, the white settlers feel the same about being displaced, same as the Utes," Lew Ron said. "For the same reasons, I suppose, its all about money; but, it is also an interesting phenomenon. Farming and ranching people have been forced out, but now there is [public] interest again in local sustainability." He referred to efforts such as the Sustainable Settings farm I mentioned earlier on Lew Ron's Great-uncle's ranch. Ironically, the news of 2008 included the story of how Sustainable Settings isn't so sustainable after all. And not because of the land. It's still rich and fertile. But current-day laws, rules and regulations make

141

it virtually impossible for the farmer to do successfully what he does—farm —
and satisfy the government's charge to provide adequate health and safety
requirements to its citizens, who, by the way, are the ones interested in sustainable living. Are we dizzy yet? "There is no stopping progress, but we're not sure
what is progress." Lew Ron said.

"We left the ranching business back in the 1970s because of more and more
rules and regulations," Lew Ron said. "Development gobbled up all the land. Not
much farming of potatoes or ranching of cattle was being done anymore. When I
was growing up, we drove cattle up from Carbondale to Marble on the road
[Highway 133]. Then there was too much traffic and we had to start trucking the
cattle up...more expense. Pretty soon, they moved our grazing lands from Marble
to Reudi (a much further, circuitous distance). We couldn't afford to run a two
hundred dollar cow on fifteen hundred dollar land for a hundred dollar calf."

LIFE GOES ON

"Everyone has to make choices what they are going to do and not do," Lew
Ron continued.

He said there are only two of the original homesteader families left in the
valley, the Thompsons and Sewells. When there was basically only agriculture
and mining, there was no other way to survive, so many families' children left
and became doctors, lawyers and engineers elsewhere.

Lew Ron's family decided to sell their six hundred acre ranch, all but for ten
acres, and with his father and brother, moved their cattle operation to British
Columbia, where there were fewer rules and regulations.

"We had three thousand deeded acres," he said of the family's Canadian
ranch, "a cattle range of five hundred square miles and [we] ran about twelve
hundred head of cattle for about fifteen years. But we found even then, it was
hard to make a living ranching anymore."

Lew Ron would come back to the homestead every winter and work in the
Coal Basin mines near Redstone or at the ski resorts in Aspen. He and one sister have stayed in the Carbondale and Glenwood Springs area. The other brother and sister have moved on.

AND EVER EVOLVES

We talked about the development of River Valley Ranch (RVR) that encom-
passes much of the original Thompson Ranch. "That was sold by the party that
bought our ranch. It is a covenant community with rules and regulations." Lew
Ron said that owners lose some independence in a regulated community; however, there is a gain of property value security. "There are two million, two and
a half million dollar homes here now."

"The early pioneers probably felt the same as the Utes did because this is a
special place, a very beautiful place to be," he said. "just trying to do whatever
one can to be here.

"Ranching and farming are nearly dead," Lew Ron said.

The Thompson cabin in Marble. Melton (not Milton) Falls in the background that can still be seen from County Road 3 at the Hermits Hideaway turnoff, across from the Marble Memorial Airport. Courtesy of the Thompson collection

"There were a number of things that changed the dynamic of the valley," he said. "RVR changed the whole dynamic. Aspen Glen (another gated community mid-valley between Carbondale and Glenwood Springs) changed the dynamic, the completed four-lane highway to Aspen changed the dynamic. It seems to be a resort community along with a second home community that drives the local economy now. There is a dramatic change in property values."

Lew Ron notes how, again, there aren't many "blue-collar" jobs in the valley anymore and the inherent vacuum created. We marvel how "affordable" housing in Carbondale is now in the four hundred thousand dollar range. What kind of "affordable" salary does that take? Add in the current economic downturn, lots of empty Carbondale storefronts and vacant new housing and the question marks get bigger.

ON A BRIGHTER NOTE

There's the flip side of what happened when a number of Aspenites began to sell and moved to these downvalley covenant communities. As with all changes, there was controversy. Heated controversy. "A lot of hell raised," Lew Ron said.

In the late 90s, elected officials voted on a referendum when new developments came to the town for building approval. First, a narrow (thirty-eight vote)

victory. Next, a period of attitude adjustment. There still is heated controversy and adjustments. Can we all say, "Marketplace?" This was a major and very contentious land development plan in Carbondale that died on the vine after numerous meetings in 2005. The acts of growth are difficult all the way around. But there are tradeoffs. There has to be good news in here somewhere, right?

"The RVR community is very philanthropic," Lew Ron said. "They support Carbondale arts and theater. Restaurants and businesses are here that wouldn't have happened."

He said his kids too have adapted and gone on into other businesses to stay in the area. One lives in the family's original carriage house adjacent to the Thompson's ancestral house built in 1889. The other son lives in Hendricks Ranch nearby. His daughter teaches school in New Castle. "You make adjustments to stay. Being 'forced out' is not a good term, it's more like 'evolved.'"

"If you want to stay, you will adapt. If not, you will go," he said. "You don't particularly like or enjoy the changes. Sure, back then was a much simpler life. It is all relative. Depends on the period of time you are in. Grandkids can't relate to that." Oh, indeed. How well the grayhairs know when the kids come to visit—with every manner of metal and satellite electronic device stuck who knows where. *Is that a stud in the middle of your tongue?*"

WHERE SEVEN GENERATIONS COME TOGETHER

"There is always a strong opposition to growth, a common trait," Lew Ron said. "The last one in the door wants to close it, but it's not very progressive and it just doesn't happen." I agree. When does the "I was here first" declaration begin? Shall we ask Cifford Duncan?

Lew Ron shared how he is concerned for his grandkids. He wants them to have opportunities to be here too. He and wife, Jackie have six grandchildren: one a senior in high school, down to seven-year-olds. The senior has already been accepted to the Colorado School of Mines and he is looking into other colleges in the engineering fields of solar, wind and civil. Not long until he, too, will be a father who comes back full circle in his family's traditions, working and living with this land on which his family has lived for over one hundred and twenty-five years. Our conversation quieted. I saw the distant look in this grandfather's eyes as he gazed towards an as yet unobstructed view of Mount Sopris.

It brings back to mind that Native American perspective … something about a grandfather saying *what we do now goes out seven generations*. Lew Ron is a man whose family of Thompsons has crossed that threshold of longevity on this land, brought round full circle in the Crystal River Valley. A deserved honor. I can't help but feel the Ute spirits here would honor these relations too.

"Talking to oldtimers is a good thing," Lew Ron said. "The historical aspect is an important part to preserve. We need to know where we came from to know where we are going. Utes, pioneers, all of us." He smiled, then said, "History is not a point in time. History is always evolving."

INDEX

Agripin,
    brother of Flavio and Sperry sheepherder, 60
Akbash
    dog, protector of sheep, 60
Arocha-Boylan, Linda, 107, 119
Aspen Daily News, 71
Aspen Glen
    gated community, 143
Avalanche Ranch, 48
Aztecas, 5

Bair, Elmer, 59, 60, 62, 79, 80
    See *"Elmer Bair's Story",* 62
    Ida, 62
Bar Fork Ranch, 35
Bascom, Gary, 126
Baumli, Esther
    See Sanchez, Esther Baumli
Baumli, Mildred, 71
Baumli, Rose
    See Wood, Rose Baumli
bears, 16, 60, 63, 132
Beaver Lake Lodge, 82, 85
Bernat, Chris, 109, 112, 113
Bernat, Kat, Jeremiah 109, 113
Bier, Jeff, 14, 15, 17, 45
Bier, Jeanette, 117

Blaine, Shaunlee and Spike, 83
Blue, June, 87
    Kirk, 88
    Sue, 52, 87, 88
Bogan Flats, 118
Bone, Peter and Becky, 117
Boylan, Bob, 119
BRB
    Campground and Crystal River Resort,
        27, 28, 29, 31, 32, 33, 43
    brother David (Graham), 91
Brown, Wayne, 119, 120, 124, 127
Budlong, Master Bobbie (photo), 131
Burkett, Bobby Raymond and Donna, 27, 30
Burkett, Raymond and Velma, 30
Burtard, Joe, Jerry and Jeff, 110

Campbell's Crusade, 91
Campbell, Larry, 90, 91
Ceretti, Carlos, 108
Chair Mountain Ranch and Cabins, 110
Chair Mountain Stables, 109-113
Chief Satanka
    or Sitting Bear, 33
Childs, Frederick, 33, 34
Church at Redstone, 89, 105
Clarence, Town of, 30, 33

Coal Basin, 46, 111, 142
Cochrane, Eva, 40
coincidences
  in the Crystal River Valley, 2, 17, 52, 55, 96, 122, 131
Coles, Mary Wood, 115
Collison, Martha, 14
Colorado Fuel and Iron (CFI) Company store, 11
Colorado Mountain College (CMC), 9, 53
Colorado Pilots Association, 52, 55
Colorado Rocky Mountain School (CRMS), 34, 35
ColoradoAerialViews.com, 37, 38, 51, 53, 138
Colorado Yule Marble Company, 75, 76
Colorado Yule Marble Mill, 76
Colson, John, 74
Community Leadership Forum (CLF), 73 , 74
Conger, Bob and Patty, 51-56
Cooper, Isaac, 33, 34
Corkie,
  Wayne Brown's church-going dog, 119
Cossins, Ira, 113
Criswell, Linda, 307
Crystal Mill, 52
Crystal River & San Juan Railway, 75
The Crystal River Pictorial, 20, 22, 47, 110
Crystal River Way Station, 109, 110, 123, 126
  See Mountain View Inn, Way Station
Crystal River Current, 76, 78, 88, 99
Crystal Valley Manor, 85, 87, 88, 89, 91, 110
curse, the Ute, 2, 10, 19, 77
Cushing, Sarah, 55

Danciger, Emma, 66, 68
dad, Ray (Graham), 79
Dave Cook Fishing Contests, 89, 91
Denver Public Library,
  Western History Collection, 4, 7, 8
Depression Days, 115, 116, 137, 140
Drake, George and Sue, 118
Duke, Doyle and Lu, 119
Duncan
  Clifford, 2, 3, 5, 7, 9, 10
  Ivan, 3
  John, 3, 7
  Willie, 3

Elk Mountain Pilot, 78
"Elmer Bair's Story", 62
Embry, Barb
  mother of Cole Wilson, 132
Emsden, Katharine, 127
Episcopalian Church, 118,
  diocese, 6, 19

Fender, Bill, 79
Ferguson, Kaye Donne, 91
Filoha Meadows, 19-25, 133
First People (Utes), 2, 7, 10, 34
Finn, Steve, 73, 127
Flavio,
  Sperry sheepherder, 60
Four Corners
  area of Southwest, 5
Freeman, John, 52
Frost, Frank, 77
Ft. Duchesne, Utah,
  Ute reservation, 3, 7

Gameskeeper's Lodge, 44, 45, 48
Gledhill, Pastor Bruce, 117
Glenwood Post-Independent, 71
Glenwood Springs Art Guild, 95
Gold Pan Gallery, 17
Grange, Joseph, 21
Grange, Kelly and Linda, 21, 22
Grant, Ulysses S., President, 80
Greer, Billy, 111, 112

H.R. Merrill, poet, 63
  See Merrill, H.R.
Hannah, Ron, 110
Hayden Drainage Map (illustration), 4
Heartbreak Hotel, 88, 89, 91, 106
Heckert, Clark, 83
Hendrix, Connie, 57, 59-62, 117, 119, 120
Hermits Hideaway
  subdivision near Marble, 52, 53, 104, 143
Herpel, Sarah, Martha, 12, 13, 14
High Country News, 71
Holden, John and Ann
  founders of CRMS, 35
Holy Cross Energy, 45
Hornsby, Jane, 16
Hunker, Rob, 37, 38, 51, 53, 138,
  See ColoradoAerialViews.com
Hunter and Game Warden story, 130

Illian, Joyce, 14, 18, 81
Inn at Raspberry Ridge, 83, 110
Isler, Rome and Ruby, 46
Italians,
  gardens, 21
  immigrants, 21, 47, 116

Johnson, Thanos, 65, 67, 69, 87
Jones, Charles R., 119

Kelly, Valery, 74, 75
Kimbrell, Pat and Hank, 82

Larson, Brad and Laurel, 120
"Leper Colony," 86
Le Van, Brook, 38-42
   Rose, 38
Lead King Basin, 47, 52, 60, 66
Leone, Bob and Miriam, 83, 126
   Luke and Abbey, 83
Lodge, Harry, 51
Lincoln Memorial, 46
Lily Lake, 21
"Little Marys," 112
Loudermilk daughters
   Raquel, Kareen, 85-87, 106, 118
Loudermilk, Wade, 51, 85, 118

Mainer, Tom and Claudette, 110- 114
Manus, Charlie, 57, 128
Man, Ben, 87
Manz, Joe, 81, 126
"Marble: A Town Built on Dreams," 31, 76, 106
Marble Age, 77
Marble Booster, 72, 76, 77
Marble Charter School, 17, 18, 66, 68, 69, 72, 73, 122-125, 127, 128
Marble City State Bank, 46, 82
Marble City Times, 76
"Marble, Colorado, City of Stone," 77
Marble Community Church, 101, 105, 106, 115-117, 119, 120
Marble High School, 121-123
Marble Historical Society (MHS), 123-125, 127
Marble mayors,
   See Brown, Wayne, 124
   See Manz, Joe, 81, 126
Marble Memorial Airport, 51, 53, 55, 85, 139, 143
Marble Meow, 77, 78
Marble Millsite Park, 46
Marble OldTimers, 110, 115
Marble Ski Area, 52, 96
Marble Times, 73
Mautz, Angelina, 41
McClaran, "Jack", 12
McClure, Gary, 13, 14
McCollum, Oscar, Jr., 31, 67, 71, 106
McCormick, Debbie and Bob, 12
McCoy, Dell, 20, 22, 47, 110
McDonald, Lucille
   third, and last wife of John Osgood, 90
McGhee Pond, 53
Meek, Col. Channing, 73, 76, 77

Meeker, Nathan, 3, 7
Meeker, the town of, 3, 5, 7
Melton
   Falls, 120, 143 *See* Milton Falls
Merrill, H.R., poet, 63
Millsite Park, 73, 123
Milton Creek, 134
Milton Falls, 139, 143 *See* Melton Falls
Mimosas-on-the-deck party, 57
Mobley, John Chester, 30-33
Moore, Ken,
   "Be Brave, Comrades," 71
Mount Sopris, 19, 20, 30, 31, 32, 34, 102, 137, 144
   See Sopris, Mount, *See* also
   We-mu-ya-ca-zus (Ute name for Sopris), 34
Mountain Dweller, 72, 74, 78
Mountain View Inn, 95,
   See Crystal River Way Station
"Mr. Eagle"
   See Hunker, Rob
Mt. Sopris Historical Society Museum, 30
Mt. Sopris Historical Society, 35
Murray, Lafe, Lori, 107, 117
Myers, Rex, 77

Nanama, "All together as One," 9
Needham, Dominique,
   Bair great-grandaughter, 62
Northern Ute elders, 2, 3 ,5, 10
Nuche
   the First People, Utes, 2, 10

Ogilby family, owners of Avalanche Ranch, 48
Ogilby, Meredith, 100
   photographer and author, *See "Women*
      of the Roaring Fork", 100
Ohnmacht, Alyssa, 16, 72, 77
Open Space and Trails,
   See Pitkin County Open Space and Trails
Orlosky, Dorothy Wood, 115
Orlosky, Marge, 88
Osgood, John Cleveland, 11, 12, 45, 90, 133

Parker, Preston, 49
Parker, Wallace, Naomi, 43-46, 48, 49, 130, 134
Petrocco, John, Ercole, 115, 116, 123
Pettijohn, Robert, Judy 132, 133, 134, 135
Pitkin County Open Space and Trails, 24, 25, 41
Placita, townsite of, 83
Prazen, Dan, 120
Preston, Joyce, 66
Puh-nit-ne ,"Open your eyes," 5

Quarrytown, 47
Razanno, Rose Baumli, 115
Red Mountain
   at Hwys 133 and 82 intersection , 34, 38
Redstone Art Center, 101
Redstone Castle, 46, 110, 111
Redstone Community Association (RCA),
   16, 101
Redstone General Store, 11, 15, 17, 18, 19
Redstone Inn, 13, 14, 48, 49, 65, 66, 81, 88,
   110, 130
Redstone Reporter, 78
Redstone Stables, 89, 110
Ritchey, Reverend Sam, 117
   Nancy, Amy and Eric, 117
River Valley Ranch (RVR) 138, 139, 142-144
Roberts, Jack
   Redstone artist, 21
Rock Creek Schoolhouse, 27, 29, 30, 31, 36
"Ruby of the Rockies," 91

Salamida, John and Karen, 55
Sanchez, Esther Baumli, 115, 123
Satank, 33, 34, 35, 36
Satank Bridge, 36
"Scenes in and about Marble Colorado," 131
Schilling, Ed, Evalyn, Gene and Steve, 89
Schilling, Mike, Judy, 89, 91, 110
Schlueter, Michael, Lisa, Victoria, Lauren, 17, 18
Schofield Pass, 30, 79, 80
   Park, 80
   Basin, 60
seven generations, 42, 144
Sewell, Sr., Bob, 28
Sewells
   original 1870s homesteaders, 40, 45, 142
sheep run, 57
Sherman Silver Act, 140
Sinnock, Duncan, 98
Smith, Ann, 86
Smith, Sylvia, 72, 76
Sneezeweeds (building), 1
Snowmass/Elk Mountain range, 2
Sopris, Mount, 19, 20, 30-32, 34, 102, 137, 144
Sperry, Joe, 59-62
Stanford, III, Bonnie and Leland, 52
Stewart, Lane
   Redstone artist, 49
Stranahan, Mike, 67
Strom, Debby, 65
Stroud, Bleu, 93, 94, 95, 97, 99
Stroud, Howard, 95

Stroud, Paul, 94, 97, 98
Sultan, Omar and Ruth, 28, 29
Sustainable Settings, 37-42, 139, 141
Swiss Village Resort, 43-45, 47-49, 130

Tabewache (Ute) band, 5
Taylor, Gloria Whitbeck, 29, 30, 32
Taylor, Nancy, 119
Tennenbaum, Gary, 25
the Angel of Love, 117, 119, 120
   marble sculpture. *See* Connie Hendrix
The Aspen Times, 71, 74
The Crystal Valley Echo, 2, 17, 72, 77
the Queen of Marble, 98
   nickname for Bleu Stroud. *See* Stroud, Bleu
The Valley Journal, 71
Thompson, Alex, 39, 40, 139
Thompson, Lewis and Julia, 139, 141
Thompson, Lew Ron, 3, 9, 137-144
   Jackie, 141, 144
Thompson, Myron, 39, 138, 139
Thompson, Tommy, 125
Thomson, John, Janet, JoAnn, 105
Thomson, David, Shirley, 82, 101-108, 119
Time Magazine, 118, 122
Tomb of the Unknown Soldier, 62
Treasury men,
   friends of Bleu Stroud, 98

Udlock, Dr. Frederick, "Skip", 106, 119
Ulysses S. Grant, 80
Updike, Katie, 119, 123, 124
Ute Curse, 2, 19
   See also the curse
Ute elders,
   See Duncan, Clifford, John,
   Willie, and Ivan
Ute words,
   Puh-nit-ne, 5
   Nanama, 9
   We-mu-ya-ca-zus, 34
Uto-Aztecan language, 6

Valle d'Aosta, 21
Vandenbusche, Duane, 77

Wagner, Patsy, 83, 109
Wagner, Gary, 109
Wagner, Robert, 126
Waite, Joyce
   Marble baker, 1
Way Station, the Crystal River, 109, 110, 123, 126

Welch, Judy, 66, 68, 97
We-mu-ya-ca-zus
 Ute name for Mt. Sopris, 34
White, David and Cathy, 117
White, O.R., 12
Whitehouse Mountain, 54, 56
Whitney, Doug, 1, 2
Wilson, Cole, 131, 132, 134
Wilson, Ken, 132
"Women of the Roaring Fork," 100,
 See Ogilby, Meredith
Woodward, Darlene, 14

yaks, 38, 41
Yampah Vapor Caves, 55
Yampatika, Ute band, 5
Yule Quarry, 46, 72,

Zorba the Greek,
 Anthony Quinn as, 65
 See Johnson, Thanos

About the Author

Ever since a small child, Charlotte Graham has loved to sit and listen to old-timers tell stories. *"Tell another bull story, Uncle Joe."* Writing has been a passion she has expressed through many venues—this is her first book. Graham lives in Marble, Colorado with her husband, Doug Whitney and their two dog children, Sam and Radar. Contact Charlotte at: www.marbledweller.com.

Made in the USA